GW01091090

A Summary of
Landlord and Tenant Law

A Summary of Landlord and Tenant Law

A. J. LOMNICKI
Dr. Iur. (Krakow), LL.M. (London)

Lecturer in Law
at the Polytechnic of
the South Bank
London

B. T. BATSFORD LTD

London & Sydney

First published 1975
© A.J. Lomnicki 1975

ISBN 0 7134 2923 2 (hard-cover); 0 7134 2924 0 (limp)

Printed in Great Britain by
Tinling (1973) Limited, Prescot, Lancs.
for the publishers B.T. Batsford Ltd
4 Fitzhardinge Street, London W1H OAH
and 23 Cross Street, Brookvale, NSW 2100, Australia

CONTENTS

vi

PREFACE

It is with hesitation that I venture to add one more to the number of books dealing with Landlord and Tenant Law but I feel there is a scarcity of texts dealing in a summary manner with this subject for the benefit of students reading for degrees and professional examinations. It is hoped, however, that the book may also be of use to professional lawyers as a short book of reference.

As Great Britain is now a member of the European Community, a short note has been added explaining the main principles of French and German legislation concerning leases.

I am indebted to my colleagues at the Polytechnic of the South Bank for their advice and encouragement and to my daughter Miss E. Z. Lomnicka B.A., LL.B., who read the manuscript and made numerous suggestions. I am, of course, fully responsible for the shortcomings which the book may still contain.

I have endeavoured to state the law as it was on 31 July 1974. The Rent Act 1974, which received Royal Assent on 31 July 1974 and came into operation on 14 August 1974 is summarized in Appendix A.

TABLE OF STATUTES.

References are to numbers of paragraphs, not pages

TABLE OF STATUTORY INSTRUMENTS.

TABLE OF CASES.

PART I

General

Chapter 1

HISTORICAL BACKGROUND AND 1925 LEGISLATION

1 Leases in Feudal Society

To discuss the historical background of any English legal concept the most convenient date to start is 1066. The effect of the Norman conquest was to introduce into England a body of administrators who were familiar with the more highly organized feudal society existing on the Continent. Although the Norman conquest cannot be said to have introduced feudalism into England (as feudalism did exist in a crude form before), yet it contributed to the development of a feudal system in England to such an extent that England became the most thoroughly feudal of all European states.

William the Conqueror fully implemented the concept that the land belonged to the Crown and that the King's subjects might only own an interest — 'an estate' — in land, whether it were a fee simple, a fee tail, or a life interest.

The 'term of years' (leasehold) has a long and peculiar history. In order to understand it, it is necessary to examine the function of the term of years in the medieval economic system. The term of years was used for purposes which in the eyes of the contemporary society were immoral and speculative, largely to evade the Church's prohibition of usury (lending money on interest). It seems that the principal object of the term of years was to enable money to be lent on the security of land at considerable profit to the lender. A moneylender would lend a sum of money to a financially embarrassed landowner. In return he took a term of years sufficiently long to enable him to recover the capital together with his profit. The tenant, therefore, was placed in very bad company among usurers and other scoundrels who preyed upon society and was not looked upon favourably by the judges administering Common Law. There was no place for tenants in the feudal hierarchy as feudal services were due from the landlord and not from the tenant.

Up to the fifteenth century a term of years was considered only as creating a contractual relationship between the owner of fee simple (landlord) and the leaseholder (tenant).

At common law only if a person possessed a legal interest (an 'estate') in land, was he entitled to sue for the recovery of the land of which he was dispossessed; such actions were called 'real actions', because they permitted the recovery of the *'res'* (thing) of which possession had been lost, ie land. If personal property was the subject of a legal action, there was no right of recovering the thing itself, but only the right of compensation for its value. Similarly, if any contract had been broken, the only remedy was damages. For this reason such actions were called 'personal actions', because they gave a right only against an individual for damages, and not the right of recovering the property. (The Chancellor sometimes intervened and, using his discretionary powers, could order specific performance of the contract instead of damages for its breach, but this matter belongs to the realm of Equity and not of the Common Law).

As a result of the distinction between real and personal actions, the term 'real' and 'personal' property arose: real property being that which was recoverable by real action (eg freehold interests in land) and personal property being that which was not recoverable itself at Common Law, but only gave the right to damages.

Because the lease was originally treated as creating a contractual relationship only, it gave no right to recovery of the land if seized, as the appropriate action was the personal action not the real action. So leases were considered personal and not real property.

Eventually leases became accepted as interests in land by medieval lawyers and by 1481 a tenant under a lease had acquired rights to recovery of the land as if it were real property. But it was too late to effect a complete assimilation of leases with real property and until 1925 on the death of the leaseholder his lease devolved under the rules of succession appropriate for personal property.

The special position of leases as interests in land was, however, recognized, by calling the leases 'chattels real'. The first word refers to their classification as personal property, the second recognizes leases as interests in land, ie estates.

2 Legislation of 1925

Before 1925, until a number of Acts simplifying real property law were passed, the complexity of estates, which might exist either at

4

law or in Equity (life interests, varieties of fee tail, fees simple and terms of years) made it a difficult and complicated task to convey real property.

It was recognised that the fewer the legal estates and interests that can exist in land, the simpler would be conveyancing and the less precarious would be the position of a purchaser.

For this reason Section 1 of the Law of Property Act 1925 has reduced the number of legal estates that can exist in land to only two, namely:

(a) an estate in fee simple absolute in possession;
(b) a term of years absolute.

The advisability of retaining in some form or other estates existing before 1925 was recognized, and those other estates may still exist, but only as equitable estates, ie as estates existing under a trust. Thus there will always by a person (a trustee) in existence, who will hold one of the two legal estates retained by the Law of Property Act and who will be entitled to transfer the legal estate vested in him.

Equitable interests existing under a trust are either registered in a land charge register (if their existence depends on the land in question), or are 'overreached' on sale, ie attached to the purchase money; this happens if the rights of the beneficiary under the trust may be satisfied by using the purchase money.

Apart from the two legal estates mentioned above (which are estates involving possession of land), there is the possibility of creating five other interests or charges in or over the land, which do not involve possession of the land, such as easements, rent charges, charges by way of legal mortgages, etc. They may be held either in fee simple, or for a term of years by analogy to the to legal estates in possession.

It is necessary to consider what is meant by the expressions 'fee simple absolute in possession' and 'term of years absolute'. A fee simple is absolute if it is neither 'determinable' nor 'conditional'. A 'determinable' fee is a fee simple which will automatically determine on the occurrence of a specified event (which may never occur). A 'conditional' fee may be subject either to a condition precedent, or to a condition subsequent. However, under Section 7(1) of the Law of Property Act 1925 as amended by the Law of Property (amendment) Act 1926, for the purpose of the Act a fee simple absolute may be subject to a certain specified condition subsequent.

The expression 'in possession' means that the estate is a present estate and not in remainder or in reversion. It includes not only the physical possession of the land, but also the receipt of rent. Thus a fee simple is considered still in possession, even though there is a tenant who has been granted a lease, as the receipt of rent is recognition that the landlord is the present owner of the fee simple.

A term of years is defined in Section 205 of the Law of Property Act 1925 as including a term for less than a year, or for a year, or years, or for a fraction of year, or from year to year. In effect term of years means a term for any period, having fixed and certain duration as a minimum, whether the tenancy will terminate at the end of that period (tenancy for a fixed period called a tenancy for years), or whether the tenancy will be automatically extended for another period, if no notice to terminate it is given by either party.

A term of years is not prevented from being absolute, by being liable to determination by notice, re-entry, or operation of law. Thus a monthly tenancy (ie a tenancy from month to month) is still absolute, even if it may be forfeited for non-payment of rent. A legal term of years, however, cannot be made for life, as it is then of uncertain duration at the time of its creation, but such an estate may exist in Equity.

Any number of legal estates may exist in the same piece of land at the same time. One person may own the fee simple and another may hold a leasehold. In such circumstances the landlord has a fee simple in possession (although he does not enjoy the land, but only collects the rent, and for this reason we may say that − loosely speaking − he is an owner of fee simple in reversion) and the tenant has a term of years in possession (and has actual enjoyment of the land).

Chapter 2

LEASES – THEIR CONCEPT

□□□

3 Leases as Chattels Real

The relationship of landlord and tenant confers on the tenant an estate in land, which may exist either at law or in equity.

A tenancy arises when one party, known as the landlord, confers on another party, known as the tenant, the right of exclusive possession of land for a period which is either subject to a definite limit, or can be made subject to a definite limit by either party.

Apart from the tenancies, which may exist by virtue of statute or by application of the doctrine of estoppel, a tenancy is created by agreement between the landlord and tenant.

Examples of tenancies created by statute are statutory tenancies under the Rent Act 1968, where a tenancy subsists not because the parties agree (as such a tenancy may exist against the wish of the landlord, who would like to get rid of the tenant), but because the statute (Rent Act 1968) protects the tenant against eviction, by granting him security of tenure, even if the contractual tenancy has come to an end. Another example is the new tenancy granted by the court under the 1954 Landlord and Tenant Act, after the contractual tenancy of business premises had expired. Also the Leasehold Reform Act 1967 allows the tenant of long lease (under certain conditions) to obtain an extension of the contractual tenancy for an additional 50 years even against the wish of the landlord.

It is also worth noting that some tenancies may be accepted by the court as in existence by applying the doctrine of estoppel. Thus if a person grants a lease without authority and afterwards becomes the owner of a superior estate in the same land (thus being authorized to grant the lease), he cannot deny the existence of the lease granted by him at the time when he was not entitled to do so.

Apart, however, from these exceptional situations, the usual way in which a lease is created is by agreement. As, however, by the tenancy agreement a legal estate, namely a leasehold, is created, such

7

an agreement creates more than only a contractual relationship.

It should be realised that a lease, once created, has a dual meaning: on the one hand it is a contract, creating a number of rights and duties binding the contracting parties *in personam,* on the other hand it is an estate in land, creating rights and duties of the parties *in rem.* A right *in personam* is enforceable only against specified parties (ie in this context persons with whom the contract has been made); a right *in rem* is enforceable against the whole world. Therefore the tenant can enforce his right to the land in question not only against the original landlord, with whom he made the contract, but also against the landlord's successor in title.

There are some legal consequences of this duality; for instance this is the reason why leases are not terminated by frustration, as other contracts are, and this duality has also its effect on the duties and rights of the parties after the lease is assigned by either. Both problems are discussed later (in Chapters 12 and 11 respectively).

The creation of leases by agreement is dealt with in Chapter 5.

Chapter 3

LEASES AND LICENCES DISTINGUISHED

4 Licences

It is of paramount importance to distinguish between a licence and a lease. This distinction is vital for many reasons, especially since, generally speaking, only leases are within the scope of social legislation protecting tenants (some occupational licences of furnished rooms, however, may be protected under Part VI of the Rent Act 1968. See § 76 (Luganda v Service Hotels Ltd 1969).

A licence permits the licensee to do some act on the land belonging to the licensor, but does not create any estate or interest in land. It simply allows the licensee to act in a manner which, but for the licence, would amount to a trespass. If the licence is possessory, ie gives the possession of land to the licensee, its affinity to a lease is clear.

There are three main categories of licences:

(a) gratuitous or bare licence;
(b) licence coupled with the grant of an interest;
(c) contractual licence.

A bare licence is a licence granted without any valuable consideration and as such is revocable at any time, as there is no valid contract between the parties; nevertheless a licensor must give reasonable notice of the revocation and in some circumstances the licensee may be entitled to damages if no reasonable notice has been given (Facchini v Bryson 1952).

A licence coupled with the grant of an interest is eg a licence to enter the land in order to enjoy an existing *profit à prendre*. Such a licence is irrevocable, as it would amount to a derogation from the grant.

A contractual licence is a licence created by a valid contract and so with a valuable consideration. Examples of such licences are cinema tickets, or those whereby guests are accepted by hotels or boarding houses, etc. The revocation of such a licence is usually a breach of contract and so gives the right to damages. Whether it is revocable is a debatable matter, as may be illustrated by the following three cases: In Wood v Leadbitter (1845) the purchaser of a ticket was ejected from a racecourse contrary to the conditions of the contract. He sued for assault, but failed, as the court accepted that the licence was revocable (but, of course, in breach of contract) and once the licence had been revoked, the plaintiff became a trespasser. He would have succeeded, of course, had he claimed damages for breach of contract. In Hurst v Picture Theatres Ltd (1915) the plaintiff, ejected mistakenly from the cinema during the performance (in breach of contract, as he had a valid ticket) sued in assault and succeeded. The Court accepted as a matter of construction of the contract that the licence was irrevocable during the duration of the performance. The Court held that in such circumstances specific performance would be available, and so the defendant was not a trespasser. Therefore the defendant committed assault by ejecting the plaintiff. The weakness of this case lies in the fact that a specific performance was not yet ordered by the court when the assault was committed. In a more recent case, Thompson v Park 1944, the owner of a school permitted another school to enter and use the premises for a consideration. This licence was revoked due to differences between the two headmasters, apparently in breach of contract. The Court of Appeal decided, that even on the assumption that the revocation had been in breach of contract, the licensee became a trespasser. The contract in this case was considered not specifically enforceable ('you cannot specifically enforce an agreement for two people to live peacefully under the same roof'). In the Court's opinion 'the owner of the house was entitled to withdraw the licence, although it may be that he would be liable in damages, if the withdrawal of the licence was a breach of the contract'.

5 Leases and Licences

Sometimes it is not easy to distinguish between a lease and a contractual licence. As a lease must always give exclusive possession to the tenant, it was probably correct law at one time to say that the right of exclusive possession was a decisive factor showing that the transaction created a lease; now, however, it is possible for a licence to have the right to exclusive possession. In deciding whether a grant amounts to a lease, or only to a licence, regard must be had to the substance rather than to the form of the agreement. In the case Cobb v Lane (1952) Lord Denning said: 'the question in all these cases is one of the intention: did the circumstances and conduct of the parties show that all that was intended was that the occupier should have a personal privilege with no interest in land?'

Thus the arrangement that 'bombed out' people should occupy a cottage rent-free for the duration of the war was accepted as a licence in Booker v Palmer (1942). It appears that a person to whom exclusive possession is granted in terms applicable to a licence will be a mere licensee, where the grant is made out of generosity, or as a matter of family arrangement (Facchini v Bryson 1952).

Although the test of exclusive possession is not decisive, it is always of paramount importance. Therefore the letting of a concert room for four days for the purpose of giving a concert was held to be a licence (as the owner retained the control of the premises). Other examples of licence are: letting space for a stall during an exhibition, a theatre refreshment contract (even if the theatre management is called 'landlord' and the restaurateur 'tenant'), accepting guests to a hotel, boarding house or furnished rooms. The last category creates some difficulty. If the room is let in such a manner that the lodger does not have exclusive possession of his room, then he is only a licensee, not a tenant; but if he has a separate apartment over which the landlord retains no control, he is a tenant.

An employee who occupies premises owned by his employer may be either a service tenant or a service licensee. He will be a licensee if he is required to occupy the premises for the better performance of his duty. This means that the need for residence in the house must arise from the nature of the servant's duties. If the employee lives in the premises belonging to the employer only as a matter of convenience to all parties, he becomes a tenant, although his landlord is also his employer.

Chapter 4

VARIETIES OF LEASES

Before discussing leases within the meaning of the Law of Property
Act it is advisable to give a short account of two types of tenancies
which do not fall into this category, namely tenancies at sufferance
and tenancies at will.

6 Tenancy at Sufferance

A tenancy at sufferance arises where a person who has held land
by a lawful title continues in possession after his title has terminated
without any statutory right to retain possession (as a protected
tenant has under the Rent Acts) and without either the agreement
or disagreement of the persons then entitled to the property. A
tenant at sufferance has no legal estate in the land, and may be sued
for 'use and occupation of land', but not for rent (which cannot be
due from him, as he is not a real tenant); further suing for rent may
be interpreted as an acknowledgement that he is a proper tenant.

7 Tenancy at Will

A tenancy at will is a tenancy under which the tenant is in
possession of the land and which is determinable at the will of either
the landlord or the tenant. A tenancy at will arises by contract
binding both landlord and tenant, and such a contract may be either
express or implied. In the case of an express contract rent may be
reserved; in the case of an implied tenancy the acceptance of rent
would generally make the tenant a tenant from year to year in the
absence of any stipulation to the contrary, as acceptance of rent is
evidence (albeit not conclusive) that a periodic tenancy has been
created. A tenant at will, however, has no estate in land, as such a
tenancy is not a 'term of year absolute' in the meaning of the Law of
Property Act 1925 (as duration not certain).

Tenancies at will are not favoured by the courts and in modern
times are not frequent. Examples of such tenancies are: entry on

land pending the completion of a contract to purchase; entry on land during negotiation for a lease; or lawful tenant holding over after the expiration of the lease with the consent of the landlord, but without creating a new tenancy.

8 Periodic tenancies

Leases within the meaning of the Law of Property Act 1925 may be either periodic tenancies (periodic yearly tenancies are called 'tenancies from year to year') or tenancies for years. Both types may exist at law or in Equity.

Periodic tenancies are included in the definition of a term of years absolute in the Law of Property Act 1925 and, consequently, the tenant of such a tenancy has as interest ('estate') in the land. Such a tenancy may be a weekly tenancy, or monthly tenancy, or a tenancy for any other continuing period chosen by the parties. It may be created by express agreement or by implication. A periodic tenancy arises by implication – presumption of law – if a person being in possession of the premises with the consent of the landlord pays rent with reference to a periodic holding. Acceptance of rent by the landlord (in the absence of rebutting evidence) is evidence that a periodic tenancy has been created.

Periodic tenancies continue until determined by a notice to quit, which, subject to any stipulation to the contrary and to statute (tenancies protected by the 1968 Rent Act are subject to special provisions) should be given so as to expire at the end of any current period of the tenancy, and must be of a length equal to the period of the tenancy.

Thus a weekly tenancy requires a week's notice, a monthly tenancy a month's notice, a quarterly tenancy a quarter's notice, but the longest period of notice required by the Common Law is six months; thus yearly and longer periodic tenancies require only six months' notice. The Agricultural Holdings Act 1948, however, provides for a year's notice to terminate agricultural tenancies.

9 Tenancy for Years

A tenancy for years is a tenancy for any period, the commencement and duration of which are certain. A tenancy for years determines at the expiration of the term without the necessity of giving any notice.

10 Squatters

The legal position of squatters deserves a short note, as occupation of vacant premises by 'squatters' is a frequent occurrence. Desperate, homeless persons resort to self-help and occupy empty houses, creating a problem for the owners.

A squatter is a person who, without any colour of right, enters on an unoccupied house or land, intending to stay there as long as he can (McPhail v Persons, Names Unknown, 1973, Bristol Corporation v Persons, Names Unknown, 1974).

A squatter has no possession of the land, unless the owner acquiesces to his presence. He is simply a trespasser and as such may be evicted by the owner, who can use reasonably necessary force to effect eviction. Although the law thus enables the owner to take the remedy into his own hands, this is not a course to be encouraged, because of the disturbance which may follow. The owner is entitled to go to court and obtain an order that the owner 'do recover' the land. There has been some difficulty when the names of the squatters are not known, but now, under RSC Ord 113 and CCR Ord 26, a summons can be issued for possession against squatters even though they cannot be identified by name and even though as one squatter goes, another comes in. The order of the court can be enforced immediately and the court cannot give any relief to the squatters, leaving it to the generosity of the owner to allow some time for the squatter to move out.

Chapter 5

CREATION OF LEASES

11 General

A lease, unless created by statute or by estoppel (Chapter 2) comes into existence as a result of an agreement between the parties.

Such an agreement may take one of the two forms:

Firstly, the agreement may of itself create a lease in favour of the tenant and convey the estate to him. Such an agreement vests the estate in the tenant immediately, although the commencement of the lease may be postponed to a future date. Rather confusingly the agreement creating the lease is also called a 'lease', and it depends purely on the context whether 'lease' denotes the estate created, or the agreement creating the estate.

Secondly, the parties may bind themselves one to grant, and the other to accept the estate in the future. Such an agreement does not create the estate immediately, but only imposes on the parties an obligation to implement the lease in the future. If the agreement for a lease is one of which specific performance will be granted (and this is usually the case), the parties are, for most purposes, in the same position as if the lease had already been granted. For this reason it is accepted that such an agreement for a lease is also a way in which a lease can be created.

Whether an instrument operates as a lease agreement (ie creating the estate immediately), or as an agreement for a (future) lease, depends on the intention of the parties, which must be ascertained from all relevant circumstances.

12 Tenancies Created by Conveyance ('Lease Agreements').

The general principle is that all leases must be created by a document under seal (ie by deed) in order to create a legal estate for the benefit of the tenant. Possession of the land (ie beginning of the lease) may be postponed to a future date — but no longer than 21 years (Section 149(3) of the Law of Property Act 1925).

The exception to this principle is contained in Section 54 of the Law of Property Act 1925. A lease may be created without any formality (ie in writing under hand only, or even orally), under the following three conditions:

(a) it must be for a term not exceeding three years; periodic leases, if the initial period does not exceed three years, are within this category;

(b) it is to take effect in immediate possession ('immediate possession requirement'); this condition is obviously imposed in order to avoid troublesome disputes over whether an oral contract has been concluded or not;

(c) it is at the best rent reasonably obtainable, without taking a 'fine' (meaning a premium). It seems that this condition has been introduced to make it more difficult for the landlord to cheat his creditors.

A lease for a term exceeding three years, or not fulfilling other conditions mentioned above, must be under seal; if, however, it is not under seal, it may be nevertheless construed as an agreement for a lease under the doctrine of Walsh v Lonsdale, discussed in § 17.

13 Tenancies Created by Agreement for a Lease

An agreement for a lease means a contract to create a legal estate at a future date. In order to be effective it must comply with all the conditions for a valid contract (there must be an intention to create legal relations, the parties must have full capacity to contract and the contract must not be tainted by illegality or any other factor which may vitiate the contract). The concluded contract must contain all the essential terms of the lease relating to:

(a) the identification of the landlord and the tenant ('parties');
(b) the premises to be leased ('subject matter');
(c) the commencement and duration of the lease;
(d) the rent or other consideration to be paid.

Any other terms, if not agreed by the parties, are implied by the law as the 'implied covenant of the leases'. These covenants are discussed later in §§ 16-26.

14 Section 40 of the Law of Property Act 1925

In addition there is a requirement in respect of the form of such an agreement introduced originally by the Statute of Frauds 1677, and repeated in Section 40(1) of the Law of Property Act 1925, which reads: 'No action may be brought upon any contract for sale or other disposition of land or any interest in land, unless the agreement upon which such action is brought, or some memorandum or note thereof, is in writing and signed by the party to be charged, or by some other person thereunto by him lawfully authorised'.

This Section applies to the creation of leases, as they are interests in land. As many leases are created by agreement for a lease and as it is important that such agreements should be enforceable, the implications of this Section should be well understood.

The effect of non-compliance with the Statute does not make the contract void, but merely unenforceable by action. The defendant must plead Section 40 expressly in order to avoid liability under the agreement.

A 'note or memorandum' need not be in any particular form, or contained in a single document in order to satisfy the requirements of the statute. It may be prepared at any time after the contract has been concluded, provided it is done before the court action has started. Several documents (even if none of them contains all the necessary terms of the contract) satisfy the requirements of Section 40 if they refer to one another in an unequivocal manner and if taken together they cover all the necessary terms of the future lease. Even a letter expressing an intention of repudiating the parol agreement, may be accepted as a sufficient memorandum (Bailey v Sweeting 1861).

It is an adequate signature for the purpose of the Act if the name or even only the initials of the party to be charged appear on any part of the document. The requirement is that it must be inserted in order to authenticate the whole document.

As the document needs to be signed only by the person 'to be charged' it is possible that the agreement will be enforceable against the party who signed the document, but not against the other party, who did not.

15 Doctrine of Part Performance

The strict application of the requirement that there must be at least a note or memorandum may cause injustice to a party who, believing in the validity of the informal agreement, incurs some expenses.

Rawlison v Ames (1925) is an excellent example of such a

situation. The defendant agreed to take a lease of a flat from the plaintiff for 21 years. The letters which passed between the parties were insufficient to satisfy the requirements of the Statute of Frauds (now Section 40 of the Law of Property Act 1925). The flat was part of a house owned by the plaintiff which was in the course of conversion and redecoration. At the defendant's request and in many cases under her direct supervision, alterations were made in the original plan for conversion. The flat was not ready by the date on which she required it and she refused to take the lease. An action by the plaintiff for specific performance succeeded. Thus possible injustice to the landlord was avoided by the application of the doctrine of 'part performance'. Although there is no memorandum of an agreement for a lease (or for any other disposition of land) such as to satisfy the requirements of the statute, yet if the agreement has been partly performed, parol evidence of it may be given in an action for specific performance. Such evidence must clearly establish that there is, in fact, a concluded agreement the terms of which are certain and definite and that there has been part performance by the party seeking to enforce the contract. For this purpose the act of part performance relied upon must be unequivocally referable to some agreement and be consistent with that alleged.

The traditional view in this respect is well illustrated by the case Madison v Alderson (1887). The plaintiff relied on promises by her employer that if she continued to work as his housekeeper (without wages) for the rest of his life, he would leave her a life interest in Manor House Farm. The appellant continued to work in that capacity until her employer's death, but the Court refused to grant specific performance of that agreement, as there was no evidence of a contract *concerning the master's land*, as alleged by the plaintiff.

In a recent case, however, (Steadman v Steadman 1973) the Court of Appeal by a majority considerably extended the scope of the doctrine. The interesting facts of the case are as follows: the parties were married in 1962. In 1963 a house was bought and conveyed to the husband and wife jointly. After their divorce in 1968, there was a dispute between them about arrears in maintenance due from the husband and about the ownership of the house. In 1972 (outside the Magistrates Court dealing with their dispute) they agreed orally that the wife would transfer her interest in the house to the husband for £1500 and that the arrears of maintenance (some £194) would be remitted for £100 which the husband undertook to repay within a month. The husband paid £100 in time, but when he asked his ex-wife to execute the conveyance of her interest in the house, she refused to do so, without payment of £2000 and not £1500 as agreed. The Court of Appeal held that the oral agreement was a contract for the disposition of an interest in land within Section 40 of the Law of Property Act 1925 and that the husband's payment of £100 was, in the circumstances, unequivocally referable to an agreement between the parties and, therefore, a sufficient part performance, even though the act of part performance was not referable to the term relating to the disposition of an interest in land. Leave to appeal to the House of Lords was given.

The following acts have been accepted as sufficient part performance:

(a) entry into possession and expenditure of money in improvements in pursuance of the agreement, or even entry into possession alone;

(b) expenditure of money in alterations by a tenant already in possession where the expenditure is not obligatory on the tenant under the existing lease (but, of course, it must be done with the landlord's knowledge and approval);

(c) payment of rent at an increased rate by a tenant in possession.

However, the mere retention of the possession by itself after the contractual lease has terminated is not sufficient part performance of any extended lease.

16 Remedies for Breach of an Agreement for Lease

If an agreement for a lease is broken, the injured party always has a right to damages, as in the case of a breach of any other contract, but this remedy cannot be obtained by a party who cannot produce an enforceable agreement, but only relies on the doctrine of part performance. This doctrine, although recognised by Section 40(2) of the Law of Property Act 1925, is an equitable doctrine and therefore only the equitable remedy of specific performance is available, and not damages, which is the Common Law remedy.

Specific performance is a discretionary remedy (available both to parties injured by a breach of an enforceable contract complying with Section 40 and also to those relying on the doctrine of part performance). Although a discretionary remedy, it is usually granted

19

in respect of a breach of contract for a lease, as, generally speaking, damages are not considered an adequate remedy. Specific performance will not be granted, however, if for any reason it would be inequitable to grant it. Thus, for example, specific performance will not be granted if the agreement is uncertain in any material respect or if its enforcement would involve undue hardship to the other party.

17 Doctrine of Walsh v Lonsdale

Leases for a period exceeding three years, which require a deed for their valid creation, pose a problem if they are in writing but not under seal. Here we are faced with a clear case of a variance between the Common Law and Equity. The Common Law requires a deed for the validity of such a lease; Equity is ready to treat such a lease as an agreement for a lease, and, if appropriate, to grant a specific performance of such an agreement. This is illustrated by the case of Walsh v Lonsdale (1882), which was decided shortly after the Judicature Act 1873 came into operation. In this case the plaintiff agreed to take a lease of a mill for seven years and part of the written agreement was that a deed should be executed containing *inter alia* a provision that on any given day the landlord may require the tenant to pay one year's rent in advance. No deed was executed; the plaintiff who was let into possession paid rent quarterly, but not in advance, for a year and a half. The landlord then demanded a year's rent in advance and upon refusal distrained for the amount. The plaintiff brought an action to recover damages for illegal distress and for specific performance of the agreement for a lease, ie the lease implied by law by the letting into possession and paying rent quarterly. The main ground upon which he rested his claim was that, as he had been let into possession, and had paid rent under an agreement, but one which did not operate as a lease (being not under seal), he was in the position of a tenant from year to year and held the mill upon such of the agreed terms as were consistent with a yearly tenancy. The condition making a year's rent payable in advance was obviously inconsistent with a yearly tenancy which could be determined by a six months' notice, and for this reason, it was argued, the distress was illegal.

This argument did not prevail. It was decided that a tenant who held under an agreement for a lease of which specific performance would be decreed, occupied the same position *vis-à-vis* the landlord as regard mutual rights and liabilities as he would occupy if a formal lease under seal had been executed.

But it cannot be said that an agreement for a lease is as good as the lease itself. The doctrine of Walsh v Lonsdale is excluded if the agreement is one of which Equity will not grant specific performance, which is a discretionary remedy. Thus in Coatsworth v Johnson (1885) the plaintiff entered into possession under an agreement that the defendant would grant him a lease for 21 years. Before the rent was due or had been paid, the defendant gave him notice to quit and evicted him on the grounds that he was in breach of a covenant contained in the agreement and intended to be inserted in the lease. The plaintiff sued in trespass, but failed, not being protected by Equity, as he did not 'come with clean hands', as one of the equitable maxims required.

Chapter 6

IMPLIED COVENANTS

18 General

Strictly speaking covenants are obligations under seal by one or other party to the lease. Since, however, many leases are created informally (eg those under three years, or those created by agreement for a lease) nowadays, in everyday life, any obligation in a lease is called a covenant.

Covenants are either express or implied. Express covenants are those covenants which have been clearly expressed and agreed between the parties. Implied covenants are those which are implied by law in default of express agreement by the parties.

In addition 'usual covenants' deserve mention. These are the covenants which are not implied in every lease, but are implied if the parties agree to create a lease 'under usual covenants'. In these circumstances all implied covenants are accepted as binding, but, in addition, some more covenants are implied.

It should be clearly understood that implied covenants are implied by law, but only unless express covenants decide the matter otherwise, because generally speaking contracting parties are allowed to regulate their obligations as they wish, although there are some covenants implied by statutes out of which the parties cannot contract. This means that they are binding even against the wishes of the parties. Some such covenants, eg in respect of liability of repair of the lease premises, will be discussed later.

Some covenants are implied on the side of the landlord (ie imposing on the landlord some obligations), some on the side of the tenant.

The following covenants are implied by the landlord:

19 Covenant for Quiet Enjoyment

Under this covenant the landlord covenants that he is entitled to grant some tenancy and that the tenant will enjoy quiet possession

22

without interruption by the landlord or by the lawful acts of anyone claiming through him or under him. This means that any successor in title of the landlord (whether *INTER VIVOS* or *MORTIS CAUSA*) is bound by the lease; however the covenant in its implied form does not impose liability on the landlord for acts of persons claiming by title 'paramount'; such a covenant must be expressly stated. Thus under the implied covenant an undertenant for a term longer than the residue of the head term has no remedy against his immediate landlord if the undertenant is evicted at the expiration of the head term. So the covenant in its implied form is not satisfactory from the point of view of the tenant, as it does not give him full protection. In properly contracted agreements it should be extended by express covenant so as to apply to the acts of persons rightfully claiming by title paramount.

An example of the application of the covenant for quiet enjoyment is the case of Markham v Paget (1908): the plaintiff was the tenant and the defendant the landlord of Styffynwood Hall. A mine nearby had earlier been let by the defendant to a third person. This mine was in use after the lease of the Hall and subsidence caused by the working of the mine resulted in damage to the Hall. It was held that the defendant had made an implied covenant to give the plaintiff quiet enjoyment of the Hall and that this covenant had been broken by the defendant when the third person (claiming through the defendant) caused the subsidence.

This covenant protects against substantial interference with the ordinary enjoyment of the premises (eg when the landlord omitted to repair a culvert on adjoining land with the result that the escape of water damaged some of the demised buildings). But it does not protect from the unlawful act of a stranger, as it is the tenant's responsibility to defend himself against trespassers.

20 Derogation from Grant

A landlord may not 'derogate from his grant', that is, do anything which is inconsistent with the purpose for which the demised premises are let. The lessor 'having given a thing with one hand, is not to take away the means of enjoying it with the other'.

In the case Aldin v Latimer, Clark Muirhead & Co (1894) the premises had been leased for the purpose (known to the landlord) of timber storage and it was held a derogation from his grant for the landlord to obstruct the flow of air necessary for drying the timber

23

by building on adjoining land. It was not a breach of the covenant for quiet enjoyment, as it was not an interference with *ordinary* enjoyment of premises, but the tenant's remedy was successfully to allege derogation from the grant, which protects the tenant's *special* use of the premises.

But a landlord, who let business premises, was held in a Canadian case not to have derogated from his grant when he let nearby premises to a competitor (Clarke Gamble of Canada v Grant Park Plaza 1967). Also, where it is found as a fact that all that the tenant has suffered is interference with amenities, relief is not to be given (Kelly v Battershell 1949). But a landlord may not use his adjoining land so as to interfere by reason of vibration with the stability of the demised premises (Grosvenor Hotel Co v Hamilton 1894).

21 Warranty for Fitness

In the absence of an express provision there is no implied covenant by the landlord that the demised premises are fit for any particular purpose with the following three qualifications:

(a) there is an implied term at common law in the letting of furnished premises that they are fit for human habitation at the beginning of the tenancy;

(b) there is a statutory implied term in certain lettings of houses at low rent that the premises are and will be kept by the landlord fit for human habitation;

(c) there is a statutory implied term in lettings of houses under 7 years duration that the landlord is responsible for certain repairs.

The whole problem of maintaining the premises in repair during the tenancy will be dealt with in Chapter 10.

The following covenants are implied by the tenant:

22 Rent

To pay rent if it is reserved. The whole problem of rent will be discussed in Chapter 9.

23 Rates and Taxes

If nothing is said in the contract, rates should be paid by the tenant (there are no taxes at present due from the land). If, however, the rent is described 'inclusive', this means that the rates are the landlord's responsibility.

24 Using the Premises

It is the tenant's obligation to use the premises in a tenant-like and proper manner. This covenant will be discussed later together with the problem of maintaining the premises and repairs (Chapter 10).

25 'Not to disclaim the landlord's title'

If the tenant by word or action denies the landlord's title and this fact is clearly established, the covenant is broken and the lease is terminated. Examples of disclaiming are the delivery of possession of the premises to a third person to enable him to set an adverse title. In our present regulated society this covenant is of rather theoretical significance, but in medieval times, when titles to land were often doubtful, it was important.

A recent example occurred when the problem of disclaimer was raised in the Courts in the case Wisbech Parish Council v Lilley (1956); an old man, who was the tenant of a cottage of which the landlord was Wisbech Council, purported to sell the cottage to a third party, and the latter was let into possession. The Council claimed that this constituted a denial of the Council's title. The Court found that the old man was genuinely unaware of the existence of the lease, despite the fact that he had paid a nominal rent since 1914. It was held that the absence of an intention to deny the landlord's title resulted in the failure of the landlord's claim.

This kind of disclaimer should be distinguished from disclaiming of a lease by a trustee in bankruptcy if the tenant became bankrupt. Where the tenant becomes bankrupt, leaseholds forming part of a bankrupt's property vest in the trustee. The trustee may disclaim leases with onerous or unprofitable covenants. A person injured by the operation of disclaimer can prove in the bankruptcy for the amount of his loss.

26 Delivery of Possession of Premises at the Termination of the Lease

It is an implied covenant by the tenant to deliver up possession at the end of the tenancy in the same condition as demised, fair wear and tear excepted. This covenant is again connected with the problem of repair and will be discussed in Chapter 10.

Chapter 7

USUAL COVENANTS

27 Usual Covenants explained

Apart from implied covenants, there is another group of covenants called 'usual covenants'. These covenants are not implied by law in all leases, but are implied if the parties state in the agreement that the lease has been created 'under usual covenants'.

It is a question of fact in each particular case which covenants are accepted as usual. These covenants are often identical with implied covenants, but in some cases go further. The following have been held to be usual covenants in particular cases:

(a) to pay rent;

(b) to pay rates and taxes (but not those taxes, eg drainage rates, which by statute are charged on the landlord);

(c) to keep and deliver up the premises in repair;

(d) to allow the landlord to view the premises in order to inspect the state of repair;

(e) a proviso of re-entry on non-payment of rent (but not on breach of any other covenant; re-entry in these cases must be expressly reserved);

On the other hand, the following covenants have been considered by the Court and not accepted as usual in the context of individual cases; ie they must be expressly stated in order to bind the parties:

(a) to pay rent in the manner agreed;

(b) to rebuild if destroyed, or repair if damaged (as distinguished from 'keeping in repair');

(c) not to assign without the landlord's consent (Chapter 13);

(d) not to exercise a particular trade (the use of building as a public house has to be expressly allowed).

Chapter 8

EXPRESS COVENANTS

28 General

Contracting parties may insert all sorts of express covenants in the lease, but there are some covenants which are commonly inserted in leases prepared by professional advisers.

The most common examples of these covenants are:

(a) to pay rent in the manner agreed;
(b) to pay rates and taxes in the manner agreed;
(c) to repair;
(d) not to alter the premises;
(e) not to assign the lease or sublet the subject of the lease;
(f) to allow or forbid a particular trade on the premises;
(g) to pass on notices received;
(h) to surrender the subject of the lease at the end of the term
(i) an absolute covenant for quiet enjoyment.

Problems of rent, repairs, assignment and subletting will be discussed in separate chapters, as they require more extensive treatment; other covenants are explained below.

To Pay Rates and Taxes

This covenant does not require any further explanation, as it is identical with the implied covenant. The time, place and manner of payment may be described in a detailed manner by the express covenant.

To Allow or Forbid a Particular Trade

Leases of business premises often contain a covenant that only a particular trade can be carried out in the leased premises, or the covenant may be formulated in a negative form, forbidding some types of trade. It is often done if the landlord is also the landlord of adjoining premises where a particular trade is already carried on. Leases of dwelling houses frequently contain a covenant 'to use the house as a private dwelling-house only'.

To Pass on Notices Received
A landlord may be affected by a variety of statutory notices, which may be delivered at the leased premises and be binding on him. Such notices, eg Compulsory Purchase Orders or Notices to Treat are of extreme importance. It is desirable, therefore, to include a covenant by the tenant to forward any such notices immediately upon receipt to the landlord.

Absolute Covenant for Quiet Enjoyment
It has been mentioned in § 19 that the implied covenant for quiet enjoyment protects the tenant from interference by the landlord and persons claiming through him, but does not protect him against interference by a person claiming the land under a title paramount. It is obviously insufficient protection for the tenant and for this reason it is often covenanted by the landlord that he promises quiet enjoyment in absolute form and is responsible for interference also by a person claiming under the title paramount. The landlord, however, as has been mentioned, never covenants to protect against interference by a mere stranger, as it is the tenant's responsibility to defend himself against such a trespasser.

Chapter 9

RENT

29 Concept of Rent

Rent is part of the consideration which the tenant furnishes to the
landlord for the landlord's allowing the tenant to occupy the leased
premises. The rest of the consideration consists of the obligation to
perform the tenant's covenants and possibly the payment of a fine
or premium, ie a sum at the beginning of the tenancy. Rent may be
regarded as of two-fold significance: first, it is part of consideration
for the grant of possession of the premises; and second, it is an
acknowledgement made by the tenant that he possesses the land
under the lease and that his possession is not 'adverse'. Therefore, as
long as rent is paid, prescription does not run against the landlord.
For this reason rent is a necessary condition of a lease. If a lease is
rent-free, then there is no indication that the possession is not
adverse and prescription thus runs against the landlord, who, after
12 years becomes barred from succeeding in an action claiming the
property in the land (Section 4 of the Limitation Act 1939).

Thus in the case of Lynes v Snaith (1899) the owner of a cottage
permitted a woman to live in it rent-free in circumstances in which,
the Divisional Court found, she was a tenant at will. After 13 years
of occupation by the woman, the owner died. It was held that the
woman had become owner of the cottage under the Limitation Acts.

For this reason, as the consideration need not be adequate, if
somebody wants to grant a lease rent-free he should reserve a
'peppercorn rent'.

Rent may be monetary or consist of chattels or services.

In the absence of express provision, rent is payable at the end of
each year of a term of years, or at the end of each period of a shorter
periodic tenancy. Usually, however, there is an express agreement
stipulating payment of rent in advance at times provided.

It is provided by statute that a rent book must be prepared and
handed to the tenant. This applies to all (furnished and unfurnished)

tenancies of dwelling houses if the rent is payable weekly. The rent book should contain the provisions of the Housing Act 1957 against overcrowding (Landlord and Tenant Act 1962 and Housing Act 1957).

It is useful to be acquainted with some nomenclature of rent:

(a) ground rent is a low rent reserved when the land is let for a long period for building purposes and the premium (initial payment) is high, covering virtually the price of the house;

(b) peppercorn rent is a symbolic rent to prevent the Limitation Act 1939 operating against the landlord;

(c) rack-rent is a rent representing the full rentable value of the property or near it; eg the Housing Act 1957 considers rack-rent as a rent amounting to more than two-thirds of the rateable value of the premises;

d) best rent is the highest rack-rent which can be reasonably obtained;

(e) head rent is the rent paid by the head-tenant, ie the tenant who subleased the property.

In agricultural tenancies it is often stipulated that the rent is payable on 'quarter days', which means on Lady Day (25 March), Midsummer (24 June), Michaelmas (29 September) and Christmas (25 December).

Chapter 10

REPAIRS

30 Implied covenant to repair

The respective liability of the landlord and the tenant to repair the premises which are let depends chiefly upon the terms of letting. In almost every case, in practice, there is an express covenant which will govern the matter if unambiguously drafted.

Cases, however, do occasionally arise where the terms of letting are not defined and, before dealing with express covenant to repair, it will be useful to discuss briefly those cases where there is no express covenant.

The landlord, not being in possession of the property, is generally under no obligation to repair the premises. The exceptions to this rule are: at common law the obligation of the landlord in the case of furnished houses to let them in a habitable state; in addition the Housing Acts 1957 and 1961 impose some obligations in respect of repair of the premises on the landlord. The provisions of these Acts will be discussed later (§ 32).

The tenant also has no obligation to repair the premises; he is generally considered only to be under an implied obligation to use the premises in a tenant-like manner and deliver them up to the landlord at the termination of the tenancy in the same state as when let, reasonable wear and tear excepted.

The tenant's obligations have been described by Lord Denning in the following words (Warren v Keen 1953): 'Apart from express contract, a tenant owes no duty to the landlord to keep the premises in repair. The only duty of the tenant is to keep the premises in a husband-like, or what is the same thing in a tenant-like manner. It can, I think, best be shown by some illustrations. The tenant must take proper care of the premises. He must, if he is going away for the winter, turn off the water and empty the boiler; he must clean the chimneys when necessary, and also the windows; he must mend the electric light when it fuses. In short he must do the little jobs about the place, which a reasonable tenant would do. In addition, he must not, of course, damage the house wilfully or negligently; and he must see that his family and guests do not damage it, and if they do, he must repair it. But, apart from such things, if the house falls into disrepair through fair wear and tear or lapse of time, or for any reason not caused by him the tenant is not liable to repair it'.

31 Responsibility for Waste

In addition to any contractual (whether implied or expressed) obligation with regard to maintaining the premises or repairing them, the occupier of land, having a lesser estate than freehold (eg tenant for life or leaseholder) may also be liable for waste. Waste may be defined as any act which alters the nature of the land. If the act causes unlawful damage to land and buildings whereby the value of the property is depreciated to the detriment of the person who is entitled to immediate reversion or remainder, the tenant is liable.

This is a tortious liability, independent of any express or implied covenant and is imposed on any limited owner, not only the tenant holding the land under a lease.

The old common law interpretation and punishment for waste was most severe and any alteration in the character of the property, even if it was an improvement, was held to be waste. For instance in the case Cole v Forth (1672) a conversion of a manual mill into a horse mill and pulling down a brew house and erecting a cottage, whereby the rent was raised from £120 to £200 was held to be a waste, although a 'meliorating' waste.

Waste may be of two kinds, either voluntary or permissive. Voluntary waste is an offence of commission, and consists of doing damage to the premises. Examples of voluntary waste are: pulling down a house, altering its structure, destroying or removing landlord's fixtures, converting meadow land into arable, cutting down trees, depositing rubbish etc.

Permissive waste is an offence of omission or negligence, that is, permitting something causing damage to the premises to happen, which the tenant is bound by the law to prevent. Examples of permissive waste are: allowing a building to fall for want of necessary repairs, allowing the fence round the park to decay whereby the deer in the park are dispersed, or allowing a breach in a sea wall to increase so that the land is flooded.

As the common law attitude to waste was extremely troublesome for limited owners in that it did not allow them to use the land to their best abilities, an estate was often granted without 'impeachment for waste' which meant that the tenant was not liable for any waste whatsoever. This was stated in the case of Lewis v Bowle in 1625. To prevent an unconscientious abuse of power given to the tenant in such cases, the Court of Chancery began to intervene and to grant injunctions to restrain the tenant from committing extreme acts of damage. Such gross damage is called 'equitable waste'. Pulling down or dismantling a mansion house, cutting down ornamental trees, are examples of equitable waste.

The tenant's obligation to abstain from waste is as follows:

– a tenant for a fixed term is responsible for voluntary and permissive waste;

– a tenant under a yearly tenancy is responsible for voluntary and, to a limited but unspecified extent for permissive waste;

– a tenant under a shorter periodical tenancy is responsible for voluntary waste only.

The whole doctrine of waste is rather out of date as far as leases are concerned, because the tenant is under a much stricter responsibility to use the premises in tenant-like manner.

32 Landlord's responsibilities for repair under the Housing Acts

In addition to the above responsibilities under the implied covenant and under the doctrine of waste, which are both of common law origin, statutes impose on the landlord some obligations of repair in respect of some tenancies.

The statutes in question are:

– the Housing Act 1957 as amended by the Housing Act 1969;

– the Housing Act 1961.

The Housing Act 1957

Under Section 6 of the Act, in any contract made on or after 6 July 1957 for the letting of a house for human habitation at a rent not exceeding in London £80 and elsewhere £52 there is, notwithstanding any stipulation to the contrary, an implied condition that the house is at the commencement of the tenancy fit for human habitation and an undertaking that it will be so kept by the landlord during the tenancy.The same condition is implied in respect of contracts made between 31 July 1923 and 6 July 1957 where the rent does not exceed £40 in London and £26 elsewhere. For earlier contracts the rent limit is even lower.

The condition cannot be contracted out of, ie cannot be excluded by any contrary stipulation. It is not, however, implied, if the contract is not for less than three years with a stipulation that the premises should be put by the tenant into a condition fit for human habitation, and the lease cannot be terminated by either party before the expiration of three years.

The landlord has a right to enter the premises after giving 24 hours' notice in order to inspect the premises. Despite the right of entry the tenant cannot recover damages in respect of injuries caused by disrepair unless the landlord has received notice of the defect. There was some uncertainty as to this at one time, but doubts were finally resolved in 1946 in McCarrick v Liverpool Corporation. The tenant's wife fractured her leg by falling on two stone steps leading from the kitchen to the back kitchen. By reason of the condition of these steps, the house was admitted to be unfit for human habitation. The House of Lords held that the tenant was not entitled to recover special damages, because the landlord had not received notice of the state of disrepair.

Fitness for human habitation is defined by Section 4 of the 1957 Act (as amended by the 1969 Housing Act). In determining whether a house is unfit for human habitation regard must be had to its condition in respect of the following and only the following matters: repairs, stability, freedom from damp, internal arrangement, natural lighting, ventilation, water supply, drainage and sanitary convenience, facilities for preparation and cooking of food and for the disposal of waste water; and the house is deemed to be unfit if and only if it is so far defective in one or more of these matters that it is not reasonably suitable for occupation in that condition.

In addition, under Section 5 'back to back' houses erected after 3 December 1909 are also considered unfit for human habitation (with some exceptions), and, under Section 18 some underground rooms (ie the rooms, the surface of the floor of which is more than three feet below the adjoining street) are also unfit for human habitation.

Apart from this implied condition, the local authority has a duty to take administrative action against the person in control of the premises in order to induce him to render the premises fit for human habitation if it is possible at reasonable cost (otherwise a closing or demolition order will be issued). It is submitted that the tenant who

34

feels that the landlord does not fulfil his obligations under this Act, would be better advised to initiate administrative action (by reporting the facts to the local housing authority) than to rely on the covenant implied by Section 6. The administrative channel will be more effective than an action for breach of covenant.

The Housing Act 1961

Sections 32 and 33 of the Housing Act 1961 provide that in any lease of a dwelling house granted after 24 October 1961 for a term less than seven years, there is to be implied covenant by the landlord:

(a) to keep in repair the structure and exterior of the dwelling house (including drains, gutters and external pipes), and

(b) to keep in repair and proper working order installations in the dwelling house:

– for the supply of water, gas and electricity and for sanitation (including basins, sinks, baths and sanitary conveniences, but not, except as aforesaid, fixtures, fittings and appliances for making use of the supply of water, gas and electricity), and

– for space and water heating.

and any covenant by the tenant for the repair of the premises is to be of no effect, as far as it relates to the matters mentioned above.

Here again the landlord has a right to inspect the premises after giving 24 hours notice and, as in obligation under the 1957 Act, the landlord's liability to repair arises only when a defect has become patent and was made known to him (O'Brien and Another v Robinson 1973).

The county court can, if the parties concerned consent and it is considered reasonable in all the circumstances to do so, make an order authorising the inclusion in a lease of provisions which exclude or modify the repairing obligations imposed by the Act. Failing this the parties to a lease cannot contract out of the provisions of the Act.

The obligation imposed by Section 32 and 33 of the Housing Act 1961 does not depend on the amount of the rent paid.

33 Express covenant in respect of repair

A general covenant to repair obliges the tenant to keep the premises in a state of substantial repair having regard to their age and nature. However, it does not extend to the re-building of the premises as a whole if necessitated by old age or inherent defect, but it involves obligation to re-build the premises destroyed by fire, earthquake, or other similar causes. For this reason a tenant who accepts such a covenant is well advised to insure the premises even if there is no express covenant imposing such an obligation on him. Destruction by enemy action has been excluded from the obligation to repair by the Landlord and Tenant (War Damage) Act 1939.

The extent of the landlord's liability, if he accepts a responsibility for repair, is illustrated by Jeune v Queens Cross Properties Ltd (1973). The landlord covenanted 'to maintain, repair and renew the structure of the property including the external walls thereof'. The court decided that the landlord had not complied with the covenants since he had failed to reinstate a balcony situated at the front of the property in the form in which it existed prior to its partial collapse.

An interesting example of the extent of the tenant's liability is shown by the case Lurcott v Wakely (1911). A house in London, which was some 200 years old, was let for a term of 28 years. The tenant covenanted 'well and substantially to repair and keep in thorough repair and good condition all the said premises' and at the end of term to yield them up so repaired. Just before the lease expired the front wall of the house was found in dangerous state and was condemned by the county council, who required the wall to be taken down and rebuilt with a new concrete foundation, footing and damp course in accordance with the London Building Act 1894. The landlord rebuilt it after the lease had expired and sued the tenant for the cost. Both the Divisional Court and Court of Appeal expressed the view that the tenant was liable for the cost of taking down and rebuilding the wall. It seems clear, therefore, that when the tenant enters into such a repairing covenant he is bound to renew any part that cannot be otherwise repaired, whether it be a door handle, a door itself, a floor or a wall.

But the tenant is not responsible for inherent defect in the house let. Thus in Litter v Lane (1895) the house was built upon boggy soil and was 100 years old when let. Owing to the original faulty construction and the passing of time, the house got into a very bad condition and was condemned by the district surveyor. The tenant was held not liable to rebuild under the covenant 'to repair, uphold, sustain, maintain, amend and keep the demised premises'. Lord Esher in the Court of Appeal said: 'If a tenant takes a house which is of such a kind that by its own inherent nature it will in course of time fall into a particular condition, the effects of that result are not within the tenant's covenant to repair. However large the words of the covenant may be, a covenant to repair a house is not a covenant to give a different thing from that which the tenant took when he entered into the covenant. He has to repair that thing which he took; he is not obliged to make a new and different thing'.

However, if the tenant covenants 'to put the premises into repair', here he by implication undertakes to put the premises into a better state of repair than that in which he found them and to make them reasonably fit for occupation by the class of persons who could be likely to inhabit them. Age, character and locality dictate the standard of repair. But the fact that the neighbourhood has deteriorated during the tenancy does not decrease the standard of repair.

Thus in Calthorpe v McOscar (1924) a 99 years' lease was granted in 1825 of three new houses in Gray's Inn, London, the tenant covenanting to repair and to yield up in repair. In 1825 the Gray's Inn was a rural neighbourhood, by 1920 it had become a slum. At the end of the lease a dispute arose as to the standard or repair expected of the tenant. The Court stated that the relevant time for applying the 'character' and 'locality' part of the text was the beginning of the lease.

Chapter 11

ASSIGNMENTS AND SUBLEASES

34 General

Assignment of leases should be distinguished from subleases. An assignment is the transfer or conveyance by one person (be it landlord or tenant) to another of an interest possessed in land. The landlord may assign his reversion, the tenant his lease. An assignment of a lease by the tenant is a transfer of the entire interest possessed in the land assigned. The tenant may assign the entire interest either in the whole or in part of the land being the subject-matter of the lease.

Subleases arise when a tenant creates a shorter lease than that which he holds himself for a subtenant.

The person assigning a lease (or reversion) is called the assignor, and the person to whom the assignment is made is called the assignee.

In everyday language it may be said that when the landlord assigns his interest in land (ie his reversionary estate) he sells his freehold subject to the existing lease. If the tenant assigns his leasehold estate it may be said that he sells the leasehold of the property.

Every landlord and every tenant has the right to assign his reversion or his lease respectively during the duration of the lease, provided that there is no covenant against assignment. The legal consequences of such a covenant will be discussed later (§§ 38-39).

The assignment is a conveyance, ie transfer of an estate in land. A deed, therefore, is required to effect the transfer of the legal estate.

An agreement to assign a lease is within the scope of Section 40 of the Law of Property Act and, therefore, is not enforceable unless there is a note or memorandum evidencing it (§ 14).

35 Privity of contract and privity of estate

A lease is a contract, but it is unique because it creates two nexus — two ties — between the landlord and the tenant. These ties are termed 'privities'. They arise between landlord and tenant after they have contracted a lease. Firstly, there is privity of contract because they have mutual contractual obligations (as in other types of contract). Secondly, there is privity of estate existing independently of the contract and which arises by the mere fact of the same piece of land 'belonging' to two persons, or, strictly speaking, of two different estates in the same piece of land belonging to two persons: the landlord's estate being a fee simple in reversion and the tenant's being a leasehold in possession. In order to appreciate the rights and duties of the parties after assignment, the concept of the two privities should be well understood.

As long as the original lease subsists, the two privities continue between the two original contracting parties, and there is no need to distinguish them. After assignment by the tenant, however, the two privities are split. There is still privity of contract between the landlord and the assignor, but there is no privity of estate between them, because the latter privity now exists only between the landlord and the assignee.

If the lease is assigned for a second time, by the assignee of the first assignment (now, the assignor of the second assignment) then, after the second assignment, privity of contract continues to exist between the landlord and the original tenant, but the privity of estate now exists between the landlord and the new assignee (as the same piece of land is the subject of two different estates belonging to the landlord and to the new assignee). The first assignee disappears completely from the picture, as there is no privity between him and the landlord any more. There is no privity of contract, because he did not contract with the landlord; the privity of estate as between the landlord and the first assignee has now disappeared, because the first assignee no longer has an estate in the land in question.

This may be illustrated by the following three diagrams:

———— denotes privity of contract   – - - – denotes privity of estate

(a) privities before assignment:

landlord

tenant

39

(b) privities after first assignment:

```
landlord
   |
   |
tenant ———— first assignee
```

(c) privities after second assignment:

```
landlord
   |
   |
tenant ———— first assignee ———— second assignee
```

The benefits of contractual obligations are freely transferable, with the exception of those under a contract for personal services (a debtor cannot object that his creditor assigned the benefit of collecting the debt to a bank, but if somebody is entitled to personal services, he cannot assign them without the consent of the person who has to perform them, because for him it is a matter of importance to whom the services have to be performed). Section 78 of the Law of Property Act 1925 confirms this rule in respect of covenants relating to the land.

On the other hand the burdens of a contract are, generally speaking, not assignable, because for a party in the position of a creditor it is a matter of importance who is obliged to perform the contract.

A lease is an exceptional contract since assignment creates special problems, which are a direct result of the two privities co-existing in the contract of lease.

In order to understand what happens to the covenants when the lease is assigned, it should be appreciated that all covenants in leases may be divided into two categories. Some covenants 'touch and concern' the land itself or the fixtures (eg buildings) on the land; other covenants are of a personal character, and do not refer to the land which is the subject of the lease. This categorization was made in the famous Spencer case (1583). It was stated that covenants referring to the land itself or to the thing existing at the moment when the contract of lease was made (things *'in esse'*) were distinguished from covenants referring to thing not in existence yet, but which were to be created on the land in future (things *'in posse'*), eg a house to be built on the land leased. Covenants relating

40

to the things *'in esse'* bound the assignee by the very fact that the assignment had been executed. Such covenants did not even require mention in the contract of the assignment. On the other hand covenants relating to things *'in posse'* only bound the assignee if they were mentioned in the contract of assignment. If, however, covenants referred to thing not in existence and not even contemplated to be created on the land, they never bound the assignee.

This rather crude distinction was simplified and put on a more satisfactory basis by the Law of Property Act 1925. Section .79 states that the burden of a covenant entered into by the tenant or landlord relating to the land binds a legal assignee of the lease or of the reversion. Covenants which do not refer to the land are treated as personal covenants and do not bind the assignee.

The following covenants 'touch and concern the land' and as such 'run with the land':

By the landlord: covenants for quiet enjoyment; for further assurance: for renewal of the lease; allowing in certain stated circumstances deduction of rent; imposing obligation on the landlord to erect a new building in place of an old one; to provide a housekeeper to clean the flat.

By the tenant: covenants to pay rent; to pay rates and taxes; to repair; to insure; to use the house as a private dwelling only; against a particular trade; against assignment without licence; to pay a fixed sum towards redecoration in lieu of damage for fair wear and tear; to reside on the premises during the lease; to erect buildings on the land leased; in the case of land near the sea to maintain a sea-wall even if the wall is not situated on the demised land.

On the other hand the following covenants are considered to be personal only and as such do not run with the land:

By the landlord: right of re-entry should the tenant be convicted of a felony; granting the tenant the right to exercise an option to take lease of other property.

By the tenant: to build a house on land other than that which is the subject of the lease; to pay rates and taxes for land not leased, etc.

36 Assignment of the reversion by the landlord

A landlord may always assign his reversion. The contract of assignment must be evidenced in writing, as provided by Section 40 of the Law of Property Act 1925 (only then may it be specifically enforced if the Court so orders), and the assignment itself must be made by deed in order to pass the legal estate to the assignee. The benefit and the burden of a covenant entered into by the tenant which directly concerns the land passes to an assignee of the reversion unless a contrary intention is expressed in the lease or the assignment.

37 Assignment of the lease by the tenant

A tenant has the right to assign his lease if there is nothing in the lease restraining him from so doing. The assignment must, of course, be by deed in order to pass the legal estate to the assignee. The assignment, it is stressed, is a transfer of the whole period for which the tenant possesses the property, as a transfer of the property for any period shorter than that which the tenant holds would be a sub-lease and not an assignment.

It is possible, however, to assign part of the land which the tenant holds under the lease. If this is done and the assignee is accepted by the landlord, the rent will be apportioned and the assignee will be responsible for his part of the rent and for keeping the covenants running with the land. The landlord's rights cannot be affected and he can demand the whole rent from either leaseholder, unless he agreed to the apportionment of the rent. Under Section 190 of the Law of Property Act 1925 the person paying rent which it is the duty of another to pay is entitled to be indemnified by that other person.

The assignment of the lease does not prejudice the personal contract between the landlord and the assignor. The assignor, unless released by the landlord from his obligations, remains responsible for all covenants entered into when the original lease was created, as privity of contract still exists between the assignor and the landlord. The assignee, however, is bound by law to indemnify the assignor against any damage which may be suffered by him through the assignee being in default in performing the obligations which he accepted by the assignment (Section 77 of the Law of Property Act 1925).

Owing to the fact that privity of estate now exists between the landlord and the assignee, the latter is responsible to the landlord for those covenants which directly refer to the land (which 'touch and concern' it). In respect of these covenants the landlord can choose whether to sue the assignor or the assignee. On the other hand, personal covenants do not run with the land and it is only the assignor who is responsible for them.

38 Covenants against assignment, subletting, parting with possession or alteration

The tenant's covenant against assignment, etc., is usually expressed in the above form, which has a wider meaning than a covenant against assignment only.

Although this covenant is neither 'implied' nor 'usual' (see §§ 18-27) many leases contain it in one form or another. Its interpretation depends on the particular words used.

Such a covenant is strictly construed against the landlord who is responsible for its drafting and for this reason it does not refer to an involuntary assignment (ie in case of death, bankruptcy or the taking of possession in execution of judgment). The landlord may have a remedy if there is a proviso of re-entry on the occurrence of such an event. A covenant against assignment is only broken by a legal assignment of the entire residue of the lease. To prevent this, the obligation not to sublet is added which includes parting with a term shorter than the entire residue. The obligation 'not to part with possession' is also added to catch all other assignments which are not legal assignments and so which might not otherwise be covered by the prohibition. Although an equitable assignment is therefore now caught, the tenant may still allow other persons to use the premises as long as the tenant retains possession.

39 Absolute and qualified nature of covenants against assignment, etc.

The covenant against assignment may be so worded as to forbid assignment or subletting absolutely, or it may prohibit the tenant assigning or subletting unless the consent of the landlord is first obtained. The covenant as formerly worded is called an 'absolute' covenant against assignment, etc.; the covenant as latterly worded is called a 'qualified' covenant. Whichever form the restrain takes, an assignment in breach of the covenant is not void. It is effectual to vest the lease in the assignee, but the landlord may treat the forbidden assignment as a ground for forfeiting the lease, provided, of course, that the covenant against assignment is accompanied by a proviso of re-entry.

Until the Landlord and Tenant Act 1927 such a qualified

43

covenant gave the landlord an unrestricted right to refuse permission
to assign, but the 1927 Act in Section 19(1)(a) provides that every
covenant, condition or agreement against assigning, underletting,
charging or parting with possession of demised premises without
licence or consent is made subject to an implied proviso that the
consent must not be unreasonably withheld.

The tenant must not assign, etc., without asking for consent,
otherwise he would be in breach of the covenant. Consent must be
asked for, but, if it is refused and in the tenant's opinion the refusal
is unreasonable, he can do one of two things: he can proceed with
the assignment or underletting using the unreasonableness of the
refusal as a defence against a possible action by the landlord for
damages of forfeiture (as the case may be); or, alternatively, he may
apply to the Court for a declaratory judgement that the consent has
been unreasonably withheld. The second course of action is safer
from the point of view of the tenant, as once he has such a
declaration of the Court he can assign, etc., without any liability to
the landlord.

The older cases tended to accept that it was reasonable to refuse
permission only on grounds connected with the status of the
assignee. Recently, however, the Courts have adopted a less
restrictive view and consent may now be considered to be reasonably
withheld:

(a) when the personality of the assignee is objectionable for some
personal or financial reasons (Under Section 5(1) of the Race
Relations Act 1965 withholding of consent on the grounds of
colour, race, ethnic or racial origins is to be treated as
'unreasonable');

(b) when the assignee's use of the property would differ from the
original and intended use (even if not forbidden by any covenant
in the original lease) and would be detrimental to the premises
demised or other property of the lessor;

(c) when the primary object of the assignment is to provide the
assignee with a protected tenancy upon the termination of the
lease proper (Lee v Carter Ltd, 1949). This case concerned a
limited company which sought permission to assign the lease of
the premises to one of its directors, who would then have held
them under a protected tenancy.

It has been accepted, however, that the consent of the landlord is
unreasonably withheld if he refuses consent in order to get some

44

advantage for himself as, for instance, to obtain a surrender of the lease, or to prevent the assignee from giving up other premises belonging to him (the landlord).

The burden of proof is on the tenant to show that consent has been unreasonably withheld.

One type of lease, however, is freely assignable. An assignment is allowed by Section 19(1)(b) of the Landlord and Tenant Act 1927 if the lease is for more than 40 years and is made in consideration wholly or partially of the erection or the substantial improvement, addition, or alteration of buildings (and the lessor is not a Government Department, or local or public authority or a statutory or public authority company). Such a lease is deemed to be subject to a proviso to the effect that in the case of any assignment, underletting, charging or parting with the possession effected more than seven years before the end of the term, no consent or licence shall be required, if notice of the transaction is given in writing to the landlord within six months after the transaction is effected.

Thus long-term building leases are freely assignable and only 'end leases' for a remaining period of less than seven years require consent. The consent in respect of end leases is required, it is submitted, because the lessee is under an obligation (often very burdensome) to hand over the premises in the same state as let, fair wear and tear excepted, and the landlord may be prejudiced by the assignment of the end lease to a financially unstable person.

Chapter 12

DETERMINATION OF LEASES

40 Frustration

It is not possible to enumerate or to classify the circumstances in which a contract is terminated by frustration. Frustration occurs when unforeseeable contingencies prevent the attainment of the purpose of the contract intended by the contracting parties. It may be described as the 'stultification of contract by subsequent events' (Cheshire). The most common cause is the destruction of the subject matter of the contract before performance falls due. The contract of lease is, generally speaking, not susceptible to frustration, because, it should be remembered, it is not only a contract, but also a conveyance of an estate in land, which is indestructible; buildings, which may be destroyed, are only fixtures of the land.

This was decided in the case Paradine v Jane (1647). Shortly after a lease had been granted, Roundheads occupied the land. Nevertheless it was held that rent was due even for the period when the tenant was forced out of the possession.

A more recent example of the same principle is Cricklewood Property and Investment Trust Ltd v Leighton Investment Trust Ltd (1945). In May 1936 a building lease was granted to the tenant for a term of 99 years. Before any building was erected, war broke out and restrictions imposed by the Government made it impossible for the tenant to erect the shops that they had covenanted to build. In an action brought against them for the recovery of rent it was pleaded that the lease was frustated, but it was held unanimously by the House of Lords that, even if the doctrine of frustration were in some circumstances applicable to a lease, it did not apply in the circumstances in question. Some authors (Treitel) consider that the doctrine of Paradine v Jane is outdated, that the contractual aspect of the lease should have preference before the estate aspect and that, therefore, frustration of leases should be accepted in suitable circumstances, particularly in short leases.

The application of the Paradine v Jane doctrine produced an unexpected result in Denman v Brise (1949), when the plaintiff was the tenant of a house. The house was destroyed by enemy action during the Second World War. The landlord built a new house on the site of the original one. The tenant wished to occupy the new house, but the landlord refused to allow him to do so, stating that the contract of lease was frustrated by the destruction of the house. Alternatively the landlord claimed to terminate the lease by giving notice to quit. It was held by the Court of Appeal that the destruction of the house had not terminated the lease, that the notice to quit was effective, but that the tenant was entitled to the possession due to protection afforded by the Rent Acts.

But in two circumstances a contract of leases is terminated by frustration: if the land itself is destroyed (eg washed away by sea), or if the house has been destroyed due to intrinsic fault (eg defective foundations, or erection on boggy soil) or age. Accidental destruction (fire, lightning, enemy action, earthquake etc) is not included. In both circumstances where frustration does occur, the tenant is not obliged to repair the premises.

41 Termination of leases under Common Law

When considering the various methods by which the lease may be terminated at Common Law, it should be borne in mind that 'welfare' legislation protects many types of tenancies, giving tenants security of tenure and limitation of rent. However, should such statutory protection cease, Common Law principles apply and the lease may be terminated under any such principle. Hence the Common Law is still basically valid despite the superimposition of social legislation.

A tenancy may be terminated in one of the following ways:
(a) by effluxion of time;
(b) by exercise of express power;
(c) by disclaimer;
(d) by merger;
(e) by surrender;
(f) by notice to quit;
(g) by forfeiture.

42 Termination of lease by effluxion of time

Only leases for fixed periods are determined by the expiration of

47

the time for which they have been created. However, termination in this manner does not fully apply to dwelling houses, business tenancies and agricultural holdings owing to social legislation.

43 Termination of lease by exercise of express power

A lease for a fixed term of years may contain a proviso giving powers to one or either party to determine a tenancy prematurely.

44 Termination of lease by disclaimer

Disclaimer may be effected either by a trustee in bankruptcy (or liquidator of a limited company) or by the tenant himself.

Disclaimer by a trustee in bankruptcy is dealt with by the law of bankruptcy (Bankruptcy Act 1914). Generally speaking the trustee in bankruptcy may disclaim, ie end the the lease if the tenant becomes bankrupt and the trustee comes to the conclusion that the lease is onerous to the bankrupt's estate. It is, of course, a breach of the lease and the damages may be claimed by proving for them in the bankruptcy proceedings.

Disclaimer by the tenant is a breach of an implied covenant (§ 25) but in addition a tenant who commits such a breach terminates the lease. Thus the tenant can put an end to his tenancy by unequivocally denying the title of his landlord, renouncing his own character as tenant and setting up a title either in himself, or in third party. This way of termination in present orderly society is of rather theoretical significance, but in medieval times, when the titles to land were often doubtful, it had its efficacy.

45 Termination of lease by merger

A lease determines by merger when the reversion and the lease become vested in the same person and there is no evidence that the parties did not intend a merger. In this case the lesser estate (ie the lease) becomes merged in the greater estate (ie reversionary fee simple).

46 Termination of lease by surrender

A lease is terminated by surrender when the tenant yields up the term to his immediate reversioner.

A surrender may be express, or by operation of law. An express surrender must be by deed or, if the lease is under three years, in writing. A surrender by operation of law occurs when the tenant acts in a way which is inconsistent with the continuation of the tenancy. The most usual instances of such inconsistent acts are: (i) delivery of possession to the landlord, (ii) a grant of a new tenancy to the tenant, if this new tenancy overlaps with the old one, or (iii) disappearance of the tenant without leaving his address and abandoning the subject of lease. Surrender (whether express or by operation of law) when carried out, must be accepted by the landlord.

47 Termination by notice to quit

It is only in respect of periodical tenancies, that the lease may be terminated by a notice to quit. The general rule is that a notice must correspond with the period of tenancy. Thus weekly tenancy requires a week's notice, a monthly tenancy a month's notice, a quarterly tenancy a quarter's notice, but yearly tenancies require only six months' notice; this is the longest notice required by Common Law.

There are three exceptions to this general rule:

(a) agricultural holdings, under the Agricultural Holdings Act 1948 require 12 months' notice;

(b) Section 16 of the Rent Act 1957 (not repealed by the consolidating Rent Act 1968) provides that any notice in respect of a dwelling house (ie house occupied for living purposes) should be given four weeks before the end of the intended termination, even if rent is payable weekly.

(c) business tenancies are also subject to special provisions in respect of the length of service of notice, which will be discussed later (§ 95).

48 Termination of lease by forfeiture

This method of termination of leases is also called 'the exercise of the right of entry' or, more popularly, 'eviction'.

As this way of termination is available to the landlord in the case of breach of covenants, if fortified by a proviso of re-entry, it will be discussed later, amongst the remedies of the landlord for breach of covenants (§ 60).

Chapter 13

RIGHTS AND DUTIES OF THE PARTIES
ON DETERMINATION OF LEASES

49 Landlord's right to possession

When a tenancy comes to an end by whatever method the position at Common Law is that the landlord has the right to the possession of the land. The social legislation has restricted this right and, in some circumstances, extended the tenancy beyond the contractual term. However, when any tenancy finally comes to an end, it is the duty of the tenant to deliver up to his landlord vacant possession of the whole of the subject of the lease, together with all buildings, improvements and fixtures which he is not entitled to remove. If the tenant has sublet the premises or part of them, it is his duty to get rid of his sub-tenant before his own tenancy ends.

The obtaining of possession by the landlord must be peaceful as, under the Forcible Entry Act 1381, it is a criminal offence to force an entry. But even if the landlord has entered forcibly (after the lease has been terminated) and thus is liable for criminal proceedings under the Statute, yet the tenant has no civil remedy against him in respect of entry. Moreover, in respect of dwelling houses protected under the social legislation the landlord cannot recover possession against the will of the tenant unless he obtains an order or judgement of the Court. In addition under the Rent Act 1965 it is a criminal offence for anyone to harass or intimidate a person occupying premises as a residence with a view to forcing him to give up possession or to refrain him from pursuing any legal remedy open to him.

50 Tenant's right to remove fixtures

A fixture may be defined as a thing of chattel nature annexed to the land. By annexation the thing ceases to be a chattel in the legal sense and becomes part and parcel of the land itself.

Annexation is not necessarily a matter of physical attachment

50

only. The question whether annexation sufficient to convert a chattel into a fixture has been effected, is a matter as much of law as of physical attachment. The annexation itself may be direct, indirect or even constructive (examples of these three types of annexation are gate posts, which are directly annexed to the land, while the gate itself is indirectly annexed to the land by being annexed to the posts and the key to the gate annexed constructively).

Sometimes it is not easy to decide whether a chattel being on the land is a fixture or not. The true test relates to the object and purpose of annexation. The mode of annexation is the only evidence helping to decide whether a thing is a fixture or not. Thus in the case of Holland v Hodgson (1872) the following definition was given by J. Blackburn L. J: 'Articles not otherwise attached to the land than by their own weight are not to be considered as part of the land, unless the circumstances are such as to show that they were intended to be part of land, the onus of showing that they were so intended being on those who contend that they have ceased to be chattels; on the contrary, an article which is affixed to the land even slightly, is to be considered as part of the land, unless the circumstances are such as to show that it was intended all along a continue a chattel, the onus lying on those who contend that it is a chattel'.

In most cases common sense will clearly show what remains a chattel, although attached to the land to some degree, and what becomes a fixture. For instance a carpet nailed to the floor, or a picture hung on the wall, or a bookcase, or a grandfather clock secured to the wall are clearly chattels. The purpose of annexation and the nature of thing itself provides the answer. Also electric bulbs, the anchor of a ship or a tent are not fixtures. On the other hand domestic stoves and grates built into the house, chimneys, wainscotting, panelling, picture rails, fixed baths, wash basins, sinks and radiators connected with pipes, locks, bolts and bars, gas and electric light brackets and pendants are fixtures. Statues, ornaments and stone seats, merely resting on the ground, but forming a part of the architectural design of a house have been held to be fixtures.

Fixtures are divided into landlord's fixtures, which a tenant has no right to remove (even if he brought them onto the premises) and tenant's fixtures, which he is entitled to remove at the end of tenancy, provided, of course, that they had been brought by him.

It is the general rule that fixtures must not be removed ('whatever has been affixed to the land, goes with the land'). This rule,

51

however, is subject to three exceptions:
  (a) trade fixtures;
  (b) agricultural fixtures;
  (c) domestic and ornamental fixtures.

Trade Fixtures

Common Law has relaxed the rule that fixtures become part of the land in the case of trade fixtures. Thus, if the chattel has been affixed for the purpose of trade, the tenant is entitled to remove it, provided that it is a chattel perfect in itself, independently of the union with the soil, and can be removed without being entirely demolished or losing its essential character or value. This relaxation of the rule has been allowed to encourage trade and industry. Examples of trade fixtures are: machinery essential to a factory, pumping apparatus at petrol station, etc.

If removal would cause irreparable damage to the premises, then even trade fixtures cannot be removed and in any case any damage caused by the removal must be made good, as otherwise the tenant would be responsible for waste, or breach of implied covenant to surrender the premises at the end of tenancy in proper state.

Agricultural Fixtures

At Common Law (Elwes v Maw 1802) the relaxation of the general rule permitting the tenant to remove trade fixtures did not extend to agricultural holdings. However, under the Agricultural Holdings Act 1948 (consolidating in this respect the Landlord and Tenant Act 1851) the right of removal of agricultural fixtures was given to the tenant, roughly to the same extent as in the case of trade fixtures. The tenant has a duty to give the landlord one month's notice and grant him a right to purchase the fixtures if the landlord so desires; the price, if no agreement is reached, being assessed by the Agricultural Land Tribunal.

Domestic and Decorative Fixtures

Chattels which have been affixed by the tenant to the premises by way of ornament or for domestic convenience and utility are removable by the tenant, because it would not be equitable for the landlord to obtain ownership of articles which may be of great value. This is well illustrated by Spyer v Phillipson (1931). Here the tenant had a lease of a suite of rooms for 21 years. Some years before the end of the lease the tenant installed some antique panelling, worth £5000, with chimneypieces and fireplaces to match, and friezes and a false ceiling to complete the decoration. The panelling was firmly attached by screws driven into plugs into the walls. The original fireplaces were removed and in one room the cornice was taken away. Parts of the brickwork were cut away to fix the new fireplaces. The tenant died and his executors claimed the right to remove panelling, etc. The landlord objected, but the Court of Appeal decided the case in favour of the executors. It was specifically stated that all damage done by erection or removal of the fixtures had to be made good. The reason for this decision was that there was no intention on the part of the tenant that the panelling should become part of the demised premises. The proper inference was that the tenant intended to enjoy the panelling himself and not to benefit the demised premises.

Thus tapestry, mirrors, blinds or cornices are ornamental fixtures and stoves, grates, pumps, furnaces, ovens, tubs, fences, cupboards and gas fittings are examples of domestic fixtures, both types of fixtures being removable by the tenant.

Chapter 14

LANDLORD'S REMEDIES
FOR BREACH OF COVENANTS

51 Landlord's remedies for non-payment of rent – General
As there are different remedies for non-payment of rent and for a breach of other covenants, the two sets of remedies will be treated separately.

There are three remedies which the landlord can resort to if the rent is not paid:

(a) court action for recovery of rent;

(b) distress;

(c) forfeiture (otherwise called 'exercise of the right of re-entry' or simply 'eviction').

52 Action for recovery of rent
A landlord may recover arrears of rent by distress or by action. Where the lease is by deed an action for arrears of rent can be brought on the express covenant contained in the lease, or, if there is no express covenant, on the covenant implied by the reservation of rent. Similarly, where the lease is created by parol, the action can be brought on the express or implied agreement for payment of rent. When a person has been in occupation of land without an agreement fixing the rent, the landlord may bring an action 'for use and occupation', under the Distress for Rent Act 1737. This action is appropriate in cases of a tenant holding over after the contractual tenancy has ended, or where there is permissive occupation without any contract. As accepting or demanding a rent from a person in occupation of land creates by implication a tenancy, landlords must not accept rent from the tenant after terminating the lease by notice or after exercising the right of forfeiture.

In view of the provisions of the Prescription Act 1939 only six years arrears of rent can be sued for.

53 Distress – Its nature

Distress is the taking of another person's chattel without legal process as a pledge for performance of a duty. The right to distrain may arise by contract, by statute or by Common Law.

By Common Law the right of distress was given in respect of a great number of services pertaining to tenures, which are now obsolete. Of the various purposes for which distress could be made under Common Law, only two are of practical importance to-day: for the recovery of rent in arrears and for the recovery of compensation for damage done by trespassing cattle (distress 'damage feasant').

By statute it is possible to distrain for arrears in rates (a warrant must be issued by a Magistrates' Court) or taxes (the warrant must be issued by the General Commissioners – Taxes Management Act 1970).

Although the remedy of distress remains available to landlords and is still in use, it has been characterized as archaic in modern conditions.

All rents carry with them, by Common Law or statute, the right to distrain for arrears. Originally the goods were distrained only in order to give security for payment, but under the Distress Act 1689 the landlord is entitled to sell the distrained goods after five full days have expired since distress without payment of the arrears. On the tenant's written request the landlord has to wait 15 days before exercising the right to sell the goods.

Distress may be effected only by the landlord having the immediate reversion.

54 Distress – Chattels excluded from distress

The general rule is that the landlord may distrain all chattels found on the demised land. Certain articles, however, are absolutely privileged against distress by Common Law or by various statutes, while other articles are conditionally privileged. This means that they may be taken only when there are no other chattels of sufficient value which do not enjoy any privilege.

The following chattels are absolutely privileged:

(a) property of the Crown;

(b) property of persons enjoying diplomatic immunity;

(c) property in the custody of the law, ie already taken in execution. The landlord, however, may notify the bailiff about the arrears of rent and the goods distrained cannot be removed from the premises unless the party for whose benefit execution has been carried pays the landlord arrears of rent due to him up to a maximum of one year (Landlord and Tenant Act 1709). In the case of the bankruptcy of the tenant six months' arrears of rent constitute a privilege debt; the balance may be proved in bankruptcy (Bankruptcy Act 1914).

(d) property delivered to a person carrying on a public trade to be dealt with in the exercise of his trade. Examples of such property are: goods sent to a warehouse to be stored or goods sent to an auctioneer to be sold and deposited in the premises occupied by him:

(e) fixtures (because they have ceased to be chattels) even if they are tenant's fixtures and as such may be removed by him;

(f) things in actual use at the time of the bailiff's visit;

(g) clothing, bedding and tools of the tenant's trade up to the value of £50. This amount (fixed in 1963) may be increased by the Order issued by the Lord Chancellor. 'Bedding' includes whatever is used for the purpose of sleeping such as a bedstead or a mattress. 'Tools of trade' are also widely interpreted. A sewing machine hired by a husband for the use of his wife who earned money as a seamstress to help cover household expenses, was accepted as privileged under this heading. It has been held that so long as clothing and bedding have not exhausted the amount privileged, a cab used by a driver can amount to an implement of trade, and so was a piano used by a music teacher, but not a typewriter used by a commercial traveller as a sample;

(h) perishable articles. This is self-evident as the articles would become worthless before they might be sold;

(i) loose money as it is not identifiable; but money in a purse or in a box may be distrained together with the container;

(j) wild animals (but tame animals in cages or deer in a fenced park are of monetary value and may be distrained);

(k) livestock and machinery on an agricultural holding not belonging to the tenant;

(l) some other goods not belonging to the tenant. Although under the Common Law the landlord could distrain for rent on all goods found on the premises even though not the property of the tenant, some exceptions were created by the Common Law, as may be seen from points (a),(b),(d) and (k) above. In addition the

Law of Distress Amendment Act 1908 created protection under some conditions for things belonging to undertenants, lodgers and also other persons, who do not have any beneficial interest in any tenancy of the premises. But this privilege does not apply to some categories of goods of which the most important are:

— goods belonging to the husband of wife of the tenant;

— goods comprised in a hire purchase agreement (but if the agreement has been terminated by a notice given by the owner, the exception to the privilege ends and the distress would be illegal);

— goods in possession of the tenant with the permission of the true owner under such circumstances that the tenant is the reputed owner of the goods in question;

— goods of a partner of the tenant.

The following things are subject to conditional privilege, ie they can be distrained only if there is no other sufficient distress upon the premises:

(a) beasts of the plough;

(b) sheep;

(c) instruments of husbandry;

(d) the tools of man's trade (if not protected absolutely by the rule explained under (g) above).

With regard to (c) and (d) the axe of a carpenter, the books of a scholar, the kneading trough of a baker, the stocking frame or loom of a weaver have been held to be within the rule. It is doubtful whether ledgers, day-books and papers of a business or professional man fall within the exception.

It may be seen that logic is not the prime characteristic of the distinctions made as regards privilege.

55 Distress: Procedure

Leave of the Court is required in the case of protected or statutory tenancy within the Rent Act 1968 (Section 111). It is the County Court which grants this leave. The Court, with respect to any application for such leave, has the power to adjourn, stay, suspend or postpone the distress. The power is identical to that possessed in relation to proceedings for possession of a dwelling house (discussed in § 81).

The distress must be levied during the continuance of the tenancy, or within six months after the tenancy has ended, provided it is done during the continuance of the landlord's title to the premises and during the possession by the tenant of the premises from which such arrears become due.

Distress may be levied only on goods on the demised premises, there being an exception where the tenant has fraudulently or clandestinely removed his chattels. Then the landlord or his agent (bailiff) may, within 30 days after the removal of goods, seize them as a distress wherever they may be found, provided that they have not been sold bona fide and for valuable consideration to any person not privy to the fraud (Distress for Rent Act 1737).

There is a six years' limitation period for distress, but in agricultural land it is only one year (Section 18 of the Agricultural Holdings Act 1948).

A landlord may levy distress either personally or through a bailiff, who is appointed pursuant to a distress warrant issued by the landlord. No person may levy distress as a bailiff, unless certified by a County Court judge (Law of Distress Amendment Act 1888).

A distrainor may enter the demised premises to levy distress, but must do so in a legal and peaceful fashion. If subsequently evicted, he may re-enter forcibly. An outer door of the house or outhouse must not be broken open, but an inner can be broken once the bailiff is inside. An open window is a legitimate means of access for the purpose of distraining, and when partially open it may be further opened for the purpose of obtaining admission. Gates may not be broken open, or closures broken down, but the distrainor may climb over a wall or fence from adjoining premises.

After entry the distrainor may seize chattels by actually taking them into possession, or by some act in relation to them which indicates an intention to seize them. A contructive seizure may be effected in various ways. Thus it was held to amount to a seizure when the bailiff entered the demised premises and, after intimating his intention to distrain, walked round the premises and, without touching anything gave written notice that he had distrained and left specified goods there, and then went away without leaving anyone in possession. As soon as seizure is complete, the distrainor should make an inventory of the goods intended to be included in the distress and should give notice of the distress in the prescribed form, setting out the amount for which the distress is levied and the authorized fees, charges and expenses.

After seizure the distrainor impounds the goods either on or off the premises. Leaving the goods on the premises under the care of the tenant is called 'walking possession'. Distrained goods are considered to be in the custody of the Law.

A landlord may distrain against a tenant adjudicated bankrupt, but, as regards the goods of the bankrupt tenant, only for six months' rent prior to the order of adjudication. The balance may be proved under the bankruptcy like any other debt.

Originally the landlord could only impound the distrained things as a security towards the arrears of rent. The Distress for Rent Act 1689, however, gave the landlord the power to sell the distrained chattels after five days' notice (which has to be extended to 15 days on the request of the tenant). It may be sold on the free market for the best price available, but usually it is done by auction in order to avoid any complaint from the tenant that the price was not the best available. Neither the bailiff, nor the landlord can buy the distrained chattels, even if they are sold by auction.

56 Wrongful distress: Remedies

A distress may be wrongful in three situations:

(a) it may be illegal, ie wrongful at the outset. An example of an illegal distress is in respect of rent which is not due or a distress by a landlord who has parted with his reversion;

(b) it may be irregular, ie if the levying of the distress is legal, but proceedings have been conducted in an irregular manner, for instance if the bailiff performs his duties in an irregular manner, when he sells the distrained goods before five, or 15 days have elapsed as the case may be;

(c) it may be excessive, ie if the distrainor seizes more goods than are reasonably sufficient to satisfy the rent in arrears and the costs of the distress.

Remedies, which may be invoked against wrongful distress (and nowadays all three types of wrongful distress are called 'illegal') are:

(a) injunction; this, of course, is an equitable, and therefore discretionary remedy and although the court issues it quite often, such an injunction is usually granted after the person asking for it gives security for the possible loss which may be incurred by the distrainor;

(b) action for damages; this action should be brought against the bailiff, not the landlord, unless it appears (as is often the case) that the landlord authorized the wrongful act, or ratified it after it came to his knowledge;

(c) replevin; this is an ancient action to obtain a redelivery to the owner of chattels wrongfully distrained, on providing sufficient security for the rent and cost of action, and on the owner's undertaking to bring an action to determine the right to distrain without delay.

There is one interesting procedure introduced by the Law of Distress Amendment Act 1895. It has been mentioned that clothes, bedding and tools of the tenant up to the value of £50 are absolutely privileged against distress (§ 54). In order to provide a cheap and quick remedy against distress wrongful in this aspect, a court of summary jurisdiction (ie a Magistrate Court) on complaint that goods or chattels exempted from distress under the above heading have been taken, may, by summary order, direct that the goods and chattels so taken be restored. If they have been sold already, the Court may direct that a sum determined by the Court, representing the value of the things sold, should be paid to the complainant.

57 Forfeiture for non-payment of rent

A lease may contain a proviso (often called a forfeiture clause) allowing the landlord to terminate the lease and re-enter on the occurrence of specified breaches of contract by the tenant. Such specified breaches do not make the lease void, but only voidable and it is up to the landlord to exercise his option to determine the lease if he wishes.

The forfeiture clause for non-payment of rent is not an implied convenant, but it must be expressly reserved in the lease. It is usually inserted in shorter leases, but not in long, building leases, as in these leases the premium (capital payment) is high and covers virtually the cost of the building, and the rent itself ('ground rent') is comparatively low and may be easily realized by other means (action for recovery of rent or distress).

It has long been settled that equity will provide relief against a forfeiture clause for non-payment of rent, whenever appropriate, considering the proviso of re-entry a mere security for obtaining the rent.

At Common Law a demand for rent was necessary before invoking the forfeiture clause, but, under the Common Law Procedure Act 1852, a landlord is not required to serve a demand if rent is six months in arrears and there are insufficient goods to be distrained. This same Act provides for more extensive relief. Even if proceedings for forfeiture have already been initiated, the tenant may stay all further proceedings by paying the arrears of rent and costs to the landlord or to the court. Moreover, there is a further discretionary remedy for the tenant. Even if judgment and execution have been obtained against the tenant in an action for ejectment for non-payment of rent, the tenant can nevertheless proceed to ask for relief in equity within six months after the date when execution was issued. But, if the court considers that the tenant has been guilty of unreasonable delay in applying for relief, the judge may well refuse relief, particularly if the landlord has incurred expenses in maintaining the premises or has agreed to re-let them to a new tenant.

Under Section 11 of the Rent Act 1968, an application for possession of a dwelling house may be adjourned or postponed and the execution stayed or suspended by the court, or an order may be issued conditionally, or after being issued rescinded on application of the tenant.

This extremely wide discretion means that in practice the County Court in an action for ejection can make the following decisions:

(a) the judge may simply adjourn the case in order to give the tenant time to pay arrears;

(b) he may grant possession on condition that the tenant pays the current rent and some additional sum towards arrears; this is an effective measure, as it compels the tenant to pay not only arrears by instalments, but also the current rent if he wants to avoid eviction;

(c) he may grant possession, not immediately, but after a fixed period in order to give the tenant time to find other accommodation.

58 Landlord's Remedies for Breach of Other Covenants than Non-Payment of Rent

The landlord had two remedies for breach of a covenant other than non-payment of rent:

(a) action for damages, which is available to the landlord whenever a covenant is broken;

(b) forfeiture (action for re-entry). This remedy is not implied, but must be expressly reserved in the lease.

59 Action for Damages

The most common covenant which gives ground for an action for damages is the covenant to repair the premises by the tenant. In such cases, in the absence of the proviso for re-entry, this is the only remedy; specific performance will not be granted for the simple reason that supervision is extremely difficult, as the standard of repair is a matter of opinion.

When the action for damages is brought by the lessor, the measure of damages depends on the following circumstances:

If the action is brought during the currency of the lease, the damages amount to the diminution in the value of the reversion, which results from the breach. It would not be fair to the tenant to adjudicate the amount necessary to put the premises into repair, for the landlord is not bound to expend money necessary to put them in repair, nor can he do it without obtaining the tenant's permission.

If the action is brought after the termination of the lease, the old rule was that the measure of damages was the sum it would take to put the premises into repair. Now, however, it is provided by Section 18 of the Landlord and Tenant Act 1927, that the damages must in no case exceed the amount by which the value of the reversion is diminished. Thus no damages are recoverable if the premises are to be shortly pulled down, or if the repairs covered by the covenant are for any other reason valueless to the reversion.

Damages for breach of any other covenant amount to the loss resulting from the breach, in accordance with the rule in Hadley v Baxendale (1854).

60 Forfeiture (Action for Re-Entry)

In an exceptional case re-entry may be sought upon the conviction of the tenant under the Sexual Offences Act 1956 for allowing the premises to be used as a brothel. The landlord is entitled to require the tenant to assign the lease to a person approved by the landlord (this approval must not be unreasonably withheld). If the tenant fails to assign within three months, the landlord may determine the lease.

Apart from this the right of re-entry must be reserved in the agreement.

Before the right of re-entry can be enforced the landlord must serve on the tenant a notice under Section 146 of the Law of Property Act 1925. The notice must specify the breach, give reasonable time for remedy of breach if at all possible and demand damages, if appropriate.

The notice under Section 146 must be drafted with caution. The demand in the notice must reasonably correspond to the obligations in the covenant which have been broken. If the notice demands anything in excess of the obligations in the covenant, the whole notice must be struck down as bad.

This is illustrated by the case Guillemard v Silverthorne (1908). (At that time the Conveyancing Act 1881 contained identical provisions to Section 146 of the Law of Property Act 1925). The notice in this case set out the general covenant to repair, and then two further special painting covenants which the lease did not contain. The notice annexed the schedule of jobs to be done, some of which were not required by the general covenant. In these circumstances the whole notice was held to be bad.

In another case, however, (Silvester v Ostrowska 1959) a notice to remedy the breach of covenant to repair also alleging the breach of a non-existent covenant against subletting was held to be good.

It is not necessary to give detailed specifications of the work to be done. Thus in the case Fox v Folly (1916) a row of houses was subject to one lease and to one repair covenant. The Section 146 notice stated that the covenant to repair had been broken and dealt with the repairs required under various headings, such as 'roofs', without specifying which particular house or houses were referred to. It was held by the House of Lords that sufficient information had been given to satisfy (what is now) Section 146.

When the landlord, after serving the requisite notice, is proceeding to enforce his right of re-entry, the tenant has a right to apply to the court for relief. The court has full discretion to grant or refuse relief and it may do so on such terms as to costs, expenses, damages, compensation, penalty or otherwise, including an injunction to restrain any like breach in the future, as the court thinks fit in the circumstances of each case.

Section 147 of the Law of Property Act 1925 provides a special form of relief in respect of the covenant to perform internal decorative repairs. The tenant may apply for relief and the court, if satisfied that the notice requiring decoration is excessive or unreasonable in all the circumstances, including the length of the tenant's term remaining unexpired, may relieve the tenant wholly or partially from liability for such repairs.

63

A forfeiture, whether for non-payment of rent, or for a breach of another covenant is presumed to be waived by the landlord if he acknowledges the continuance of the tenancy for the period after the forfeiture. Accepting rent which has accrued since the forfeiture, distraining for such a rent, or suing for it amounts to waiver to the right to forfeit. Such an acceptance of or demand for the rent for the period after the forfeiture, even under protest or 'without prejudice' amounts to a waiver (Segal Securities Ltd v Thoseby 1963, Central Estate (Belgravia) Ltd v Woolgar N.2. 1973).

PART II

Social Legislation Protecting Tenants

Chapter 15

HISTORICAL OUTLINE

61 Scope of Social Legislation

Since 1915 when the first 'Increase of Rent and Mortgage Interest (War Restrictions) Act' was enacted, social legislation protecting tenants has been with us in one form or another and it is certain that this protection will be with us for many years to come, if not for ever.

'Social legislation' (as it used to be called) protects three types of tenancies, albeit in different ways. These tenancies, as defined by the Acts, taken together, cover virtually all tenancies which exist in present society. They are tenancies in respect of dwelling houses, business premises and agricultural holdings.

In all three types of tenancies protection entails the limitation of rent and security of tenure. These two kinds of protection have to go together, because limitation of rent would be of little value for the tenant if the landlord were able to terminate the tenancy at will; similarly, security of tenure would not be worth much to the tenant if not accompanied by the limitation of rent. In addition, in business tenancies and agricultural holdings it is very important to encourage the tenants to improve the premises in order to make the businesses (or the agricultural holdings) as efficient as possible and for this reason in respect of those two types of tenancies it is provided that the tenant (under specified conditions) may claim compensation for improvements made by him, provided they enhance the value of the premises.

In addition there are a number of ancillary provisions in respect of dwelling houses which either give the tenant additional protection, or ensure that he will not be subject to devious stratagems of the landlord (these include the obligatory issue of a rent book, the giving of extended periods of notice to terminate the tenancies, provisions against 'harassment' and the conferring of wide discretion to the Court to grant reliefs, etc).

Thus this subject will be dealt with under the following headings: firstly, historical outline, as only by tracing the history of the legislation will it be possible to understand it fully and appreciate its meaning and significance; secondly, tenancies of dwelling houses; thirdly, business tenancies; fourthly, agricultural holdings; fifthly, ancillary provisions.

A word of warning: the legislation is so complex that it can be discussed only in outline in this book. We are dealing here (as one judge picturesquely commented) with 'a jungle of legislation, sometimes ill-designed, causing endless litigations'. The student who wants to master the subject thoroughly is referred to the more detailed works listed in the bibliography at the end of the book.

62 History of the Rent Acts and Allied Legislation

Until the First World War demand and supply of houses were fairly well balanced and therefore there was no need for the Government to intervene by introducing any compulsory measures in this respect.

Only at the beginning of the War did several factors contribute to an acute shortage of accommodation in towns: the nation's effort was directed towards the production of war materials and the building of new houses virtually stopped. There was a great migration of rural population to the towns to work in factories. Houses were not repaired and maintained. The Government was anxious to maintain the value of the Pound and to fight inflation. For this reason the first Rent Restriction Act was passed as a temporary measure for the duration of the First World War. However, hopes that the shortage of accommodation would disappear after the War were not realized.

Therefore there were a number of Rent Restriction Acts passed during the First World War and between the wars, the last of them being the Increase of Rent and Mortgage Interest (Restrictions) Act 1938. This Act made several amendments and additions to previous Acts and limited the application of the Rent Acts to dwelling houses the rateable value of which did not exceed £35 in London or Scotland and £20 elsewhere. Hence on 1 September 1939 these were the only houses which remained controlled. The rent of these houses was fixed by reference to the 'standard rent', which was the rent at which the dwelling house was let on a specified date in 1915.

It was expected that during the Second World War conditions

would again create a necessity for the control of a larger number of houses and, when the war was imminent, on 1 September 1939 the Rent and Mortgage Interest (Restriction) Act 1939 was passed. This Act took under control all dwelling houses (which were not controlled under the existing legislation) the rateable value of which did not exceed £100 in London, £90 in Scotland and £75 elsewhere. As the rent restricted under the 1939 Act was referred to the rent paid in 1939, this control was called the 'new control', to distinguish it from the 'old control' under previous Acts, where the rent was referred to the rent paid in 1915.

Both controls were retained after the Second World War and, as a result of statutory limitations imposed on rent, many houses were let at rent which bore no relation to the open market value of the houses. In consequence, landlords were either unwilling, or unable to keep their houses in repair. This contributed considerably to a number of houses becoming unfit for human habitation and to the spreading of slum properties, particularly in larger towns.

To remedy this state of affairs the Rent Act 1957 was passed.

The Act markedly reflected the policy of the Conservative Government of that time. It decontrolled all houses whose rateable value (as assessed in 1956) exceeded £40 in London and £30 elsewhere. A new system was introduced for those houses left under control, namely a 'rent limit' instead of the previous 'standard rent'. The 'rent limit', generally speaking, was considerably higher than the 'standard rent'. However, the Housing Act 1957 (see § 32) imposed on the landlords the obligation to keep houses where rent was very low fit for human habitation.

The 1957 Rent Act marks the beginning of the end of controlled tenancies. It was intended to tolerate controlled tenancies as a temporary, albeit long time, expedient, because:

(a) tenancies created on or after 6 July 1957 (date when the Rent Act 1957 come into operation) were not controlled even if they otherwise came within the scope of the Act;

(b) houses converted or erected after 30 August 1954 were exempted from control (Housing Repairs and Rent Act 1954);

(c) only one 'succession' was allowed; the second succession would not be protected.

(d) the Minister, by statutory instrument (subject to affirmative resolution of both Houses of Parliament) might decontrol houses in a given locality, or lower the rateable value governing protection. Needless to say, this power has never been exercised.

On the coming into power of the Labour Government in 1964, a determined attempt to reverse the philosophy of the 1957 Rent Act was adopted. The Rent Act 1965 considerably extended the scope of protection and attempted to produce a more flexible and sensible policy in respect of rent. The existing provisions of the Rent Acts down to 1957 were left virtually as they were and controlled tenancies were left to die out slowly as envisaged by the 1957 Rent Act. A new concept, a 'regulated' tenancy, was introduced, to which every tenancy (not being controlled under the 1957 Act — either because the rateable value exceeded the prescribed limits, or because the tenancy commenced after 5 July 1957, or the house was erected or converted after 30 August 1954, or because the tenant and his first successor had died), of a dwelling house was subject, the rateable value of which on 23 March 1965 did not exceeded £400 in Greater London or £200 elsewhere.

The security of tenure for both groups of tenancies, ie controlled and regulated, remained virtually the same (with a few rather unimportant differences which will be mentioned in due course), but rent was restricted in quite a different manner, being in regulated tenancies a 'fair rent'. The regulated tenancies were visualized as a long-term expedient, although even so it was provided that if scarcity of dwelling houses should disappear in any area, the Minister (now Secretary of State for the Environment) might by Order provide for partial or total exemption from protection of dwelling houses in that area.

After the 1965 Rent Act was enacted, the law governing protection of dwelling houses became so complicated that on 8 May 1968 a new Act, the Rent Act 1968, was passed, which did not change the existing law but consolidated the provisions of the previous Acts. However, some of the previous Acts retained their validity, as the consolidation did not embrace the whole problem of protection of dwelling houses. The Rent Act 1968, with later amendments (Housing Act 1969, Housing Finance Act 1972 and the Counter Inflation Acts 1972 and 1973) is now the basic Act dealing with protected tenancies of dwelling houses.

Shortly after enacting the 1968 Act, the Government reached the conclusion that the slender resources available for building purposes would be put to better use if they were directed towards the repair and improvement of existing houses rather than the building of new ones.

The Housing Act 1969 in realizing this policy arranged for the extension of financial assistance towards the costs of improvement and conversion on a much more general scale than previous legislation. Such assistance was in certain circumstances automatic and not dependent on local authorities' discretion (this was the case with improvements providing 'standard amenities'). In order to induce landlords to provide houses with standard amenities (with the financial help of local authorities) it was decided that houses enjoying standard amenities (defined in Schedule 1 to the Act) might be converted from controlled into regulated tenancies. A detailed procedure (outlined later) was introduced to effect the conversion and the increase of the rent allowed as a result of the change from controlled into regulated tenancies was 'phased' by providing for five yearly instalments.

In October 1969 the Minister of Housing and Local Government appointed a Committee with the task of reviewing and reporting on the operation of rent regulation under the Rent Acts and on the relationship between the codes governing furnished and unfurnished lettings. The Labour Government who appointed the Committee hoped that it would advise that furnished tenancies be granted security of tenure similar to that enjoyed by unfurnished tenancies. The Committee, under the chairmanship of H.E. Francis QC (hence the name of the report 'Francis Report') did not recommend this, but submitting their report in March 1971 (when the Conservative Government was in office) suggested a number of changes. The most important, perhaps, was the suggestion that all controlled tenancies should be abolished and converted into regulated tenancies (ie not with the 'rent limit' but with the much higher 'fair rent') and suggested some other amendments to the Rent Act 1968, mostly directed towards benefitting landlords.

Many of the Committee's recommendations were accepted by the Government and found their way onto the Statute Books under the name of the 'Housing Finance Act 1972'.

Further, inflation and 'floating' of the Pound (which in practice has meant devaluation) induced the Government to issue two Counter Inflation Acts in 1972 and 1973. The first froze rent for dwelling houses for the five months ending 29 April 1973; the second introduced higher rateable values which limit protection of tenancies. These provisions will be discussed in due course.

In March 1974 a Labour Government came into power again.

In fulfilling their election promises they froze rent for dwelling houses (both in the public and private sector) for the period starting on 7 March 1974 and ending with the year of 1974. In addition the rent during the standstill period on re-letting any dwelling previously let within the preceding twelve months, shall not exceed the previous rent. These freezing provisions have been enacted by the following Statutory Instruments:

(a) the Counter Inflation (Public Sector Residential Rents) (England and Wales) Order 1974 S.I.381;

(b) The Counter Inflation (Public Sector Residential Rents) (England and Wales) No 2 Order S.I.434;

(c) the Counter Inflation (Private Sector Residential Rents) (England and Wales) Order 1974 No 380.

These orders only froze the rent. They did not defer the dates for the general conversion of controlled into regulated tenancies under Section 35 of the Housing Finance Act 1972 (see § 75). This has been done by two other Statutory Instruments:

(a) Regulated tenancies (Conversion from Control) Order 1973 S.I.752;

(b) Regulated Tenancies (Conversion from Control) Order 1974 S.I.615.

which postponed the conversion of controlled into regulated tenancies until 1 January 1975.

Rent for business tenancies (see chapter 22) has also been frozen from 1 December 1972 until 31 December 1974 by three Statutory Instruments:

(a) Counter Inflation (Business Rents) Order 1972 S.I. 1850;

(b) Counter Inflation (Business Rents) Order 1973 S.I.741;

(c) Counter Inflation (Business Rents) Order 1974 S.I.1030.

In June 1974 the Government indicated that the freezing of rent would end on 31 December 1974, but that the outstanding increases will be phased.

As any freezing of rent is strictly temporary measure, in discussing the provisions of social legislation, these temporary provisions will generally be disregarded, unless they have some permanent efficacy, as, for instance, the postponement of the date of conversion of controlled into regulated tenancies.

This book follows the scheme of the 1968 Act as amended by future legislation. Additional chapters deal with long tenancies, furnished lettings, business tenancies and agricultural holdings. The last two types of tenancies are protected under separate legislation in different ways and under different principles.*

Chapter 16

PROTECTED TENANCIES OF DWELLING HOUSES: PRELIMINARY

Note: In Chapters 16-20 all statutory references are references to the Rent Act 1968 unless otherwise stated.

63 Protected Tenancies

A tenancy under which a dwelling house (which may be a house or part of a house) is let as a separate dwelling is a protected tenancy, provided that its rateable value does not exceed the prescribed limits. However, some types of tenancies which are within the rateable value limits imposed by the Act are exempted from protection.

A dwelling house (be it a separate building or flat) must be let as a separate dwelling in order to be protected. A tenancy does not enjoy full protection (but will be protected to a limited extent as explained in §83) if any vital living accommodation, for instance a living room, or a bedroom is shared. However, sharing of ancillary parts, such as the hall, a lavatory or a bathroom does not deprive the dwelling of its separate character and such dwellings are fully protected. In some cases (eg the sharing of a kitchen) it is a matter of degree whether the dwelling is deemed shared or not.

The second condition is that the rateable value of the dwelling must not exceed the prescribed limits. The Rent Act 1968 in Section 1 stated simply that the rateable value must not exceed on the appropriate day £400 in Greater London or £200 elsewhere; the 'appropriate day' meant either 23 March 1965 (for the houses which were shown on that date in the valuation list), or the date on which the dwelling was first shown in the valuation list if later than 23 March 1965.

This simple rule, however, has been amended by the Section 14 of the Counter-Inflation Act 1973. The wording of the amendment is rather complex.

The criteria for protection depend on the dwelling's rateable value on the date on which it appeared in the valuation list, or on 23 March 1965, whichever is the later. This date is known as the 'appropriate day'.

(a) If the appropriate day falls before 23 March 1973 (but of course after 23 March 1965) the dwelling may satisfy any of the following three conditions in order to be protected:

(i) that the rateable value on this date did not exceed £400 in Greater London, or £200 elsewhere.

This re-states the limits imposed by the 1968 Act;

(ii) that on 23 March 1973 the rateable value of the dwelling did not exceed £600 in Greater London or £300 elsewhere. Although there was no general re-valuation between 1965 and 1973, some dwellings could have appeared in the valuation list during this period with the rateable value over £400 or £200, not because they were more valuable than the houses in category (i) but because the valuation was higher due to inflation. Thus these houses deserved higher limits.

(iii) that on 1 April 1973 the rateable value did not exceed £1500 in London or £750 elsewhere.

The increase of the limits of the rateable value was necessitated by the general re-valuation of hereditaments in Great Britain. Nevertheless it does seem to indicate a further extension of protection.

(b) if the appropriate day is between 24 March 1973 and 31 March 1973 the dwelling may satisfy either of the conditions (ii) or (iii) above;

(c) dwellings appearing in the valuation list after 1 April 1973 must satisfy (iii) above only.

If the question arises in any proceedings whether a dwelling house is within the limits of rateable value explained above, it shall be deemed to be within these limits unless the contrary is proved.

64 Statutory Tenancies

The legal problem involved in affording security of tenure to contractual tenancies even after they have ended, is solved by creating 'statutory tenancies'.

Under Section 3 a tenant, whose contractual, protected tenancy has come to an end and who remains in possession owing to the protection given by the Act (perhaps against the will of the landlord) is called a 'statutory tenant'. Both protected and statutory tenancies may be either controlled or regulated. Thus as long as the contract between the parties lasts there is a protected tenancy (controlled or regulated); once the contract is terminated by a notice given by the landlord or by the death of the tenant, a statutory tenancy arises (which may also be controlled or regulated). Thus we have four types of tenancies, but it is not necessary to distinguish between them as far as security of tenure is concerned, because all of them are protected in a virtually identical way. Small differences between controlled and regulated tenancies will be explained in due course. Similarity of protection applies only to security of tenure; the limitation of rent, however, in controlled tenancies is based on completely different principles than regulated tenancies.

Although the tenant enjoys the same security of tenure whether he is a 'protected' or 'statutory' tenant, his legal position is quite different. A statutory tenant has no estate or property in land, but merely a personal right to remain in the dwelling house. His interest is nothing more than a 'status of irremovability'; his landlord may obtain possession of the property occupied by such a tenant, but only on the court order in specified circumstances described below. A statutory tenant must occupy the dwelling house himself, or be prevented from living there by circumstances beyond his control, in which case he must evince a clear intention to return to it as soon as he can. The terms and covenants of the previous contractual tenancy (eg in respect of subletting, repairs, etc) bind the statutory tenant as if he were still a protected (ie contractual) tenant.

65 Succession

Both protected and statutory tenancies may be transmitted on the death of the tenant to members of his family (Section 3 and Schedule 1). In the case of his wife it is sufficient if she lived with her husband at the moment of his death. In the case of other members of the family of the deceased, they have had to live with him for the last six months before his death. It has been held that the members of the tenant's family include the parents, husband, brothers, sisters, children (also illegitimate), niece, illegitimate daughter of the deceased sister and even cousins.

In respect of controlled tenancies only one succession is possible; a second succession is allowed under the Act, but the second successor of a controlled tenancy becomes only a tenant of regulated tenancy, thus having security of tenure, but limitation of rent only to the fair rent level. Under the 1972 Housing Finance Act a third successor is not protected at all.

66 Subletting of Statutory Tenancies

A statutory tenant may sublet part of the premises being the subject of the lease, but he has no right to sublet the whole premises (because the subletting of the whole premises is a ground for the landlord to ask for possession of the premises).

A lawful sub-tenant (ie whose tenancy was not created in breach of the covenant in the lease) enjoys the protection of the Act against the head landlord, even if the head tenancy comes to the end, provided that:
— the head tenancy is within the Rent Act;
— the sub-tenancy, if it were a head tenancy, would have been protected (Section 18).

67 Tenancies Excluded from Protection

Not all tenancies of dwellings within the limits of the rateable value prescribed by the Act and let as separate dwellings are protected. There are some tenancies which are exempted from protection owing to either the terms of the tenancies (a) (below), or the character of the dwelling (b) and (c) below), or the status of the landlord ((d), (e) and (f) below).

Thus the following tenancies are not protected:

(a) Tenancies at a Low Rent

A tenancy is outside the Act if the rent payable is less than two-thirds of the rateable value on the appropriate day (see § 63 for an explanation of this term). As the rent may be variable, taking into account service and maintenance charges, Section 80 of the Housing Act 1969 provides that these charges should be disregarded in assessing the low rent.

The reason for this exclusion is that it is clear that the vast majority of the tenancies excluded are long building leases, where the initial payment covers the costs of the building, and the rent (the 'ground rent') represents the acknowledgment of the landlord as a reversioner, rather than being a commercial rent. As long tenancies are protected in a different manner (explained in Chapter 21), no injustice arises from this exclusion.

If the tenancy is not a long one then, if the rent is low, it is probable that the tenancy is no more than a family arrangement or for a charitable purpose. Thus no injustice arises from the complete deprivation of protection.

(b) Houses with Other Land

A tenancy is outside the Act if a dwelling house is let together with land, other than the site of the dwelling house, as long as the land is agricultural and exceeds 2 acres.

(c) Furnished Lettings

If a letting is let bona fide at a rent which includes payments in respect of board, attendance or use of furniture, it is not a protected tenancy, although it is protected to a lesser degree under Part VI of the Act. The question of furnished tenancies will be discussed in Chapter 19.*

(d) Crown Properties

Here are included the properties belonging not only to the Queen personally, but also to the Government.

(e) Local Authority Properties

Although local authorities' properties ('council houses') are not protected under the Rent Act, in practice the security of tenure of such tenancies is equivalent to the security afforded by the Rent Act.

(f) Houses belonging to Commission for the New Towns, the Housing Corporation, a Development Corporation established under the New Towns Act 1965 or housing trust

A 'housing trust' is a corporation or body of persons which is required to devote the whole of its funds to the provision of houses for persons, the majority of whom are members of working classes (Section 5 (3)).

*But see Appendix A — Summary of Rent Act 1974

Chapter 17

PROTECTED TENANCIES OF DWELLING HOUSES. SECURITY OF TENURE

□□

68 Security of Tenure
Security of tenure is virtually identical for all protected tenancies, be they 'protected' or 'statutory', 'controlled' or 'regulated'.

The landlord cannot recover possession of the dwelling house (even if it is not protected within the meaning of the Act) against the will of the tenant, unless he obtains an order of the court. (Sections 31 and 32 of the Rent Act 1965 were not repealed by the Rent Act 1968).

Under Section 10 of the Act the court shall not make an order for the possession of a dwelling house which is let on a protected tenancy or is subject to a statutory tenancy, unless the court considers it reasonable to make such an order and either:

(a) the court is satisfied that suitable alternative accommodation is available for the tenant, or

(b) the circumstances are as specified in any of the nine cases given in part 1 of Schedule 3 to the Act.

The first requirement is that the court must come to the conclusion that it is reasonable to issue the order for possession. The court has to consider a wide range of circumstances in deciding the reasonableness. No exhaustive list can be made, but the personal circumstances of the tenant are clearly to be taken into account.

In a recent case Redspray v Francis (1973) a tenant, having a flat in a quiet street, was offered, as alternative accommodation, a flat in a noisy street with a cinema and shops in the vicinity. This was not considered a suitable alternative.

Once the reasonableness has been established, the court has to consider whether condition (a) or (b) is satisfied.

The 'alternative accommodation' condition is inserted into the Act rather than the Schedule because it seems this condition is a basic one. The purpose of the Act is obviously to protect only those

79

tenants who are in need of a roof over their heads.

In order to decide whether the accommodation offered is a suitable one, the court is given the following rules (Schedule 3 Part IV):

A certificate of the local authority of the district that the accommodation is suitable shall be conclusive evidence for the court.

Otherwise the court must be satisfied that the accommodation is suitable in respect of:

(a) the size (this means that it would not be suitable if it would result in overcrowding within the meaning of the Housing Act 1957);

(b) the security of tenure (it must be either protected or with equivalent security,eg a council accommodation);

(c) the proximity to the place of work;

(d) the rent. This does not mean that the rent must be identical, but it should be suitable for the tenant's means and for the standard of the accommodation offered.

The nine cases given in Part I of the Third Schedule in which the court may give possession (if in all circumstances it considers it reasonable), are:

(a) where any rent due from the tenant has not been paid, or any obligation of the tenancy has been broken or not performed; thus the tenant can be sure that security of tenure will be afforded to him only if he performs all covenants binding him.

(b) where the tenant (or his lodgers or subtenants) commits a nuisance or annoyance or permits use of the premises for immoral or illegal purposes.

Here nuisance has a wider meaning than in the law of tort; it is used not in the technical, legal meaning, but in its everyday sense. The following examples show that annoyance has a wider meaning than nuisance: allowing the sink to overflow, making excessive noise, and even committing private sexual immorality (Whitbread v Ward 1952) have been held annoyances.

(c) where the tenant committed waste or neglected the premises or defaulted in their maintenance;

(d) where the tenant has given notice and, in consequence, the landlord has contracted to sell or let the dwelling and would be seriously prejudiced if he could not obtain possession;

(e) where, without the consent of the landlord the tenant has (after 8 December 1965 in the case of regulated and after 1

September 1939 in the case of controlled tenancies) assigned or sublet the whole of the dwelling house.

The reason for this is that if the tenant relinquishes possession of the whole premises, apparently he does not need the dwelling and if so, does not deserve protection. There may be, however, exceptional circumstances (temporary absence) when subletting may be justified and for this reason it is left to the discretion of the court to grant possession to the landlord.

(f) in off-licence premises if the tenant commits an offence as holder of the licence or conducts the business in an unsatisfactory manner. This case applies only to controlled tenancies, as mixed tenancies (business and dwelling), if not controlled, are protected by Part II of the Landlord and Tenant Act 1954, which deals with business premises.

(g) where the tenancy is required by the landlord for his full-time employee and the tenant to be evicted was, but ceased to be, in the employment of the landlord;

(h) where the premises are reasonably required by the landlord for himself, his son or daughter over 18 years of age, his father or mother or (in regulated tenancies only) for his parents in-law. Part III of the Third Schedule adds two conditions:

(i) the landlord did not buy the dwelling house in question either after 23 March 1965 (if regulated tenancy) or after 7 November 1956 (if controlled tenancy); the reason for this restriction is that after these dates the premises were already protected and the landlord buying them should have realized this.

(ii) the court must come to the conclusion that greater hardship would be caused for the landlord or his family if possession were refused, than for the tenant if possession were granted.

(j) where the tenant sublets the premises for an excessive rent, ie in excess of the amount appropriate for controlled or regulated tenancy if the subletting is one of those tenancies.

There are four circumstances (called 'cases' 10 − 13), given in Part II of the Third Schedule, where the court must order possession where the dwelling house is subject to a regulated (but not a controlled) tenancy.

The condition common to all four cases is that the landlord has to give the tenant notice that possession might eventually be recovered under the 'case' in question. The notice should be given by the 'relevant date'. This means, for tenancies created before 8

81

December 1965 (when the Act creating the regulated tenancies came into operation), 7 June 1966. In other cases it means the date of commencement of the regulated tenancy in question.

The four classes in which the court *must* grant possession are:

(a) if the court is satisfied that the dwelling house is required as a residence for the owner-occupier or any member of his family who resided with him when he last occupied the house. Here, in contrast to case (h) mentioned above, the court has no discretion to grant possession, but must do so if it is satisfied the request is bona fide;

(b) parsonage houses if they are required for occupation by the successor; (this case was applied even when the premises were not occupied by the parson himself, but let by him: Bishop of Gloucester v Cunnington 1943);

(c) houses occupied by persons employed in agriculture, if they are needed for successors in employment. In contrast to the discretion given in case (g) above, the court has no discretion in agriculture cases, as it is recognised that it is essential for efficient husbandry to have the worker living near the holding;

(d) under some conditions houses required for persons responsible for agricultural holdings if the amalgamation of farms is being carried out.

The last three cases are of limited importance, but the first should be noted. It means that it is possible to contract out of the protection, if the house is bona fide required by the landlord or members of his family in the future.

Chapter 18

LIMITATION OF RENT

69 Controlled Tenancies

As was explained in §62, the Rent Act 1957, which decontrolled a considerable number of tenancies, visualized controlled tenancies as a temporary expedient only, providing for their gradual disappearance.

The elimination of controlled tenancies has been considerably expedited by subsequent legislation. This will be discussed in some detail in the chapter dealing with the conversion of controlled into regulated tenancies, but even now it should be realised that controlled tenancies, in view of the provisions of the Housing Act 1969 and particularly of the Housing Finance Act 1972 (which introduced 'general decontrol' of the controlled tenancies) are a dying concept and, therefore, only a short note in respect of their rent limitation is included.

Before the general decontrol started (it began on 29 April 1973), controlled tenancies were those in which rateable value of the house (as ascertained by the valuation list on 7 November 1956 — § 3 of the Schedule 8 to the Act) did not exceed £40 in London and Scotland or £30 elsewhere.

In addition, as was indicated in § 54, the tenancy, in order to be controlled, had to begin before 6 July 1957, the dwelling house had to be erected or produced by conversion before 30 August 1954 and, if the original tenant had died, it has to be occupied by the first successor. If any of these conditions is not satisfied, the tenancy is regulated only.

Generally speaking the rent is limited ('rent limit') to double the *gross* value of the premises on 7 November 1956.

The 'rent limit' once it has been ascertained can be adjusted upwards only in the following circumstances:

(a) *rates*. If the landlord is responsible for rates and they have been increased, the rent limit may be increased by the amount of the difference;

(b) *adjustment in respect of services and use of furniture.* If the landlord provides any of these (and the tenancy does not enjoy the status of a furnished one), and there is an increase in the cost of providing these commodities, the rent may be increased by agreement between the parties, or, failing such an agreement, by the County Court;

(c) *improvements.* If improvements have been carried out by the landlord, he is entitled to an increase in the rent limit. For improvements which were effected between 6 July 1957 and 23 November 1961 the rent limit could have been increased by 8% of the cost, for improvements carried out since 23 November 1961 by 12½% of the costs of the improvements. If improvements have been carried out with the assistance of a grant from the local authority, only the net cost borne by the landlord may be accepted as the basis for the calculation of the increase of the rent.

The reason for increasing the percentage from 8% to 12½% by the Housing Act 1961 was that the lower amount, introduced by the Rent Act 1957, did not give sufficient inducement to the landlords to make the improvements. Even this measure, however, did not bring about the desired effect, so the Housing Act 1969 supplied further inducement by providing that a house enjoying 'standard amenities' (as defined by the Act) may be decontrolled.

70 Regulated Tenancies. Rent Limitation under the 1965 Rent Act as Consolidated by the 1968 Rent Act

Whereas security of tenure is virtually identical for all protected and statutory (whether controlled or regulated) tenancies, rent for regulated and controlled tenancies is limited in a quite different way.

Regulated tenancies are tenancies of dwelling houses whose rateable value is now under £1500 in Greater London and under £750 elsewhere. Therefore virtually all dwellings which are let unfurnished, apart from those very luxurious ones, are subject to protection.

Regulated tenancies are visualized as a permanent feature of our landlord and tenant law, although under Section 100 of the Act, if there is no scarcity of accommodation in a given locality, the Minister may issue an order providing that dwelling houses in that locality will not be subject to protection, or lowering the rateable value limits. Such an order has to be approved by both Houses of Parliament and, so far, no such order has been issued and it is not expected that one might be issued in the foreseeable future.

The rules about limitation of rent introduced by the Rent Act 1965 have been amended by the Housing Finance Act 1972. For the better understanding of these provisions, the rules, as introduced by the 1965 Act, are first explained, and the changes made by the 1972 Act are discussed afterwards.

The detailed provisions of rent limitation for regulated tenancies as enacted in 1965 (and consolidated in 1968) were rather complex; some technical distinctions were made between those contractual tenancies which existed in December 1965 (when the Rent Act 1965 came into operation) and those contractual tenancies created after December 1965, and also between contractual and statutory tenancies. As the rules were simplified in 1972 by the Housing Finance Act of that year, only an outline of the principles introduced in 1965 are here discussed.

The idea behind regulated tenancies was that all rents should be fair. This was achieved by the concept of determination and registration of fair rent by the Rent Officer.

If the rent had been registered, the fair rent was the rent as registered. If the rent had not been registered, but the tenancy had existed from before December 1965, the fair rent in respect of those tenancies is, *prima facie,* the rent paid on 8 December 1965. However, either the landlord, or the tenant, or both jointly might apply to the Rent Officer for the assessment and registration of a fair rent under the procedure outline below. If the premises had not been let on 8 December 1965 and no rent is registered, the rent limit will be the contractually agreed rent, but again with the proviso that either party, or both, may apply to the Rent Officer for determination and registration of rent.

The rent limit (ie either the rent registered, or, if not registered, the rent existing on 8 December 1965, or if not registered and not existing on 8 December 1965, as agreed between the parties) might be adjusted in some circumstances.

If the rent had been registered, the only possible adjustment was that consequent to a change in rates, if borne by the landlord.

If the rent had not been registered the rent limit may be adjusted in the following circumstances:

85

(a) any change in responsibility for repair;
(b) any change in the provisions in respect of use of furniture;
(c) any change in burden of rates (if paid by the landlord);
(d) any change in the costs of services (if provided by the landlord);
(e) any cost of improvements effected by the landlord (12½% per annum of the net cost).

71 Regulated tenancies. Determination and Registration of Rent by Rent Officers

In all cases where the rent has not been registered (or registered more than three years ago), either the tenant or landlord, or both parties jointly, may apply to the Rent Officer for the determination and registration of the fair rent. (Section 44 and Schedule 6). The application must be in the prescribed form. If the Rent Officer requires additional information from either party he can call for it. If the application has been made jointly by both parties and the Rent Officer is satisfied that the rent applied for does not exceed the fair rent, he will register it forthwith. If the application is made by one party, the Rent Officer serves a notice of the application on the other party and this party can make representations within the time given by the Rent Officer, which must be at least seven days. If no representations are received and the Rent Officer is satisfied that the rent is fair, he will register it.

If a party makes representations, or if the Rent Officer is not satisfied that the joint application states the fair rent, he invites both parties (giving them at least seven day's notice) to appear at a specified time and place before him. After the hearing (and, if necessary, after visiting the premises) the Rent Office determines the fair rent and notifies both parties.

A party may within 28 days raise objections to the determination and in this case the Rent Officer refers the matter to the Rent Assessment Committee. The Committee decides the issue after asking, if necessary, for further information and after an oral hearing, which is arranged either on the Committee's initiative, or if either party asks for the hearing. A party may appear either personally or by a representative (not necessarily a barrister or solicitor). The Committee may view the premises in the presence of both parties (or their representatives). The decision of the Rent Assessment Committee is final and may be challenged in the High

Court by applying for the Order of Certoriari (as in the case of other final judicial decisions taken by administrative tribunals or inferior courts).

Chairmen of the Rent Assessment Committees are nominated by the Lord Chancellor; the members, by the Secretary of State for the Environment.

The rent, as determined by the Rent Officer or by the Rent Assessment Committee, is registered in a register maintained by the Rent Officer. Even if registered, the fair rent is not immutable for ever. A fresh application to the Rent Officer may be made every three years or even earlier on change of circumstances.

The Act gives only very general guidance as to the way in which the Rent Officer should determine the fair rent.

In fixing the fair rent all the circumstances must be taken into account, in particular the age, character and locality of the dwelling house and its state of repair. The circumstances which must be left out of account are as follows:

(a) personal circumstances, eg the financial difficulties of the particular tenant. In 1965 it was considered that the Supplementary Benefit given by the Ministry of Health and Social Security would take care of persons not in full time employment, who would have difficulty in meeting the rent; the Housing Finance Act 1972 provides an allowance for some categories of tenants (even if they are in full-time employment) to help them meet the rent;

(b) any disrepair or defect attributable to the failure of the tenant or any predecessor in title to comply with the terms of the tenancy; the tenant cannot, by allowing the dwelling house to fall into disrepair, obtain a lower rent;

(c) any improvements (a term which includes the replacement of any fixture or fitting – Housing Act 1969 Section 83) which the tenant, or any predecessor in title has carried out except if it had been done under the terms of tenancy. If the tenant has improved the premises beyond his obligations, the benefit of his work should not increase his burden in paying rent;

(d) any scarcity element: it is provided that when determining the fair rent it must be assumed that the number of persons seeking to become tenants of similar houses in the locality is not substantially greater than the number of available houses.

This in practice the Rent Officer faces a very difficult task; the

Francis Committee in submitting their report in March 1971 unanimously praised the work done by the Rent Officers.

In performing their task the Rent Officers accept as useful evidence the rents determined as fair for lettings of comparable properties, or they calculate the capital cost of the property and a fair return on the capital spent; sometimes they look at an open market rent, deducting from it the 'scarcity value'. Each of these methods or a combination of them is used by the Rent Officers.

In a recent case, Anglo-Italian Properties Ltd v London Assessment Committee (1972), it was held by the Court that where a fair rent is determined by considering a percentage of the capital cost and the actual cost of repair, it is not appropriate to deduct a percentage for scarcity value. It is submitted that this percentage as applied takes care of the scarcity value.

72 Regulated Tenancies. Certificates of Fair Rent

It may happen that a person intends to provide a dwelling accommodation by the erection of a new house or by the conversion of existing house, or intends to make some improvements in a dwelling house already let, or let the premises for the first time, where no fair rent is determined. In these circumstances the person, before incurring expenses and before taking the final decision, might like to know what will be the fair rent which he would be able to charge.

For this reason Section 45 allows such a person to apply to the Rent Officer for a certificate (known as a 'certificate of fair rent'), which specifies a rent which, in the opinion of the Rent Officer, would be a fair rent.

Schedule 7 covers the procedure governing the application for the certificate of fair rent and the action expected from the Rent Officer. The application may refer:

(a) to a house which is not ready yet for occupation (ie a house to be built or converted); or

(b) to a house already subject to a regulated tenancy, but which is to be improved; or

(c) to a house which is unoccupied and ready for letting, but in respect of which there is no fair rent determined.

In the first and third cases (a) and (c) the application has to be accompanied with appropriate plans and specifications, and the Rent Officer after asking, if necessary, for additional information may determine the future rent. In case (b) an appropriate notice should be served on the tenant and the tenant is entitled to be present during any consultations. Either party, if not satisfied with the Rent Officer's determination, may ask for a reference of the case to the Rent Assessment Committee.

In the case (c), where the house is ready for occupation, if the Rent Officer is satisfied that the rent asked for is the fair rent, he registers it; if he is not satisfied, he considers the application in consultation with the applicant. Here again the applicant, if he is not satisfied with the determination of the Rent Officer, can refer the case to the Rent Assessment Committee.

Where a certificate of fair rent has been issued in respect of a dwelling house, an application for registration of a rent in accordance with the certificate may be made within three years.

Under Part II of Schedule 6, the Rent Officer, on receiving an application for the registration of a rent which has been determined by the certificate of fair rent has to check whether the works specified in the certificate have been carried out according to the plans and specifications submitted, or whether the condition of the dwelling house is the same as that at the date of certificate.

If he is so satisfied he registers the rent; if not, he notifies the applicant accordingly and at the applicant's request, or on his own initiative, refers the matter to the Rent Assessment Committee. The Committee, if satisfied that the works have been carried out as undertaken, will direct the Rent Officer to register the rent; if not satisfied, it will direct the Rent Officer to refuse the application for registration.

These provisions about the certificate of fair rent are useful, as they may induce owners to convert their houses into self-contained flats, or improve them, thus creating more and better houses for letting.

73 Regulated Tenancies. Changes Introduced by the Housing Finance Act 1972

Under the 1968 Rent Act rent of a regulated tenancy (whether protected or statutory) could not be increased except by redetermination and re-registration of fair rent by the Rent Officer. Even the agreement of the parties was not binding if the rent agreed was in excess of the fair rent. Section 20 provided that where the rent agreed exceeded the limits specified, the amount of the excess should, notwithstanding any agreement, be irrecoverable from the tenant.

The Housing Finance Act 1972 amended the Rent Act 1968 in several respects.

Section 41 of that Act introduced a new Section 48A to the Rent Act 1968, which allows the parties to a lease with a registered rent to make a joint application to the Rent Officer, asking him for the cancellation of the registration of a rent for a dwelling house.

The two following conditions must be satisfied:

(a) the new agreement must take effect after the expiration of three years since the last registration of rent (or since the application for the registration of a different rent if the last registration was not a first one);

(b) the new agreement must be for at least 12 months (without prejudice to the landlord's right to terminate the agreement in case of non-payment of rent or breach of the terms of the tenancy).

If the Rent Officer is satisfied that the rent payable under the rent agreement does not exceed the fair rent, he shall cancel the registration. The cancellation of the registration is without prejudice to a further registration at any time on the application of either party.

No application for cancellation of registration may have been made before 1 January 1973.

The second amendment is contained in Section 43 of the Housing Finance Act 1972. Under this Section, if the rent for a dwelling house is not registered, then the parties to a regulated tenancy, whether protected or statutory, may freely enter into an agreement as to the amount of the rent, provided that the agreement contains a statement that the tenant's security of tenure will not be affected if he refuses to enter into an agreement and that the entry into the agreement will not deprive the tenant or landlord of the right to apply to the Rent Officer at any time for determination and registration of the fair rent. This agreement (called in the Act a 'rent agreement with a tenant having security of tenure') may be made on or after 1 January 1973.

These two amendments, carrying out the recommendation of the Francis Committee Report (see §62), change the whole philosophy of the Rent Act 1968. Registration of rent ceased to be a condition for obtaining an increase in rent and has become only a safeguard for the parties (which in practice means the tenant) to avoid exploitation. This is so because the Act secures for both parties a right to apply to the Rent Officer for the determination and registration of the fair rent if they are not satisfied with the freely agreed rent.

Another amendment of some importance to the provisions of the regulated tenancies has been introduced as a result of Part II of the Housing Finance Act 1972, which imposes on the local authorities a duty to grant rent allowances to needy tenants in order to help them with payment of rent. Allowances in respect of rent for unfurnished lettings, introduced by the Finance Act 1972, were extended to furnished tenancies by the Furnished Lettings (Rent Allowances) Act 1973.

Therefore the local authorities, faced with the duty to pay rent allowances, are interested in ensuring that the rent is not excessively high. This problem has been taken care of by Section 44A of the 1968 Act (introduced by Section 29 of the Housing Finance Act 1972). The local authority may apply to Rent Officer for consideration of the fair rent for any dwelling in their area. If the Rent Officer reaches the conclusion that the rent paid by the tenant exceeds the fair rent, then he determines and registers the fair rent and the tenant has to pay only the registered rent. The landlord may ask for the case to be referred to the Rent Assessment Committee, as in all other cases of the determination of the fair rent by the Rent Officer.

74 Conversion of Controlled Tenancies into Regulated by Providing Standard Amenities

Controlled tenancies may be converted into regulated tenancies in two ways: either under the provisions of the Housing Act 1969, now amended and consolidated in the Housing Finance Act 1972 by providing the premises with the 'standard amenities', or by 'general decontrol' of controlled tenancies under Section 35 of the Housing Finance Act 1972.

It has been already mentioned (in § 62) that the Housing Act 1969 created the possibility of the conversion of controlled tenancies into regulated ones under certain conditions. This part of the 1969 Act was repealed and replaced by Part III of the Housing Finance Act 1972, which streamlined and simplified the procedure.

A controlled tenancy may be converted into a regulated one, provided that (Section 27 of the Housing Finance Act 1972):

91

(a) the dwelling is provided with all standard amenities for the exclusive use of the occupant;

(b) the dwelling is in good repair having regard to its age, character and locality and disregarding internal decorative repairs,

(c) it is in all other respects fit for human habitation.

Standard amenities are set out in Part I of Schedule 1 to the Housing Act 1969 and comprise:

– a fixed bath or shower with hot and cold water:

– a sink with hot and cold water:

– a wash basin with hot and cold water:

– a water closet.

The standard amenities must be provided for the exclusive use of the occupant. Thus, a dwelling with a shared bathroom or water closet does not possess standard amenities within the meaning of the Act.

Regarding fitness for human habitation, the Housing Act 1957 in Section 4 (as amended by the Housing Act 1969) states that in determining whether a house is unfit for human habitation, regard must be paid to its condition in respect of the following matters: repair, stability, freedom from damp, internal arrangement, natural lighting, ventilation, water supply, drainage and sanitary convenience and facilities for the preparation and cooking of food and for the disposal of waste water. The house shall be deemed to be unfit for human habitation if, and only if, it is so far defective in one or more of the said matters that it is not reasonably suitable for occupation in that condition.

Part I of the 1969 Housing Act imposes on the local authorities an obligation to pay a standard grant in order to provide financial help towards introducing the standard amenities as described above. The standard grant is usually paid only in order to provide all standard amenities and under the condition that the dwelling is likely to remain fit for human habitation for a period which is not less than 15 years.

The authority for the conversion of a controlled tenancy into a regulated one is given by the local authority by issuing a 'qualification certificate'. There are two separate procedures for cases where the dwelling already has the standard amenities and for cases where the dwelling has not yet been provided with them.

In the first case, ie if the standard amenities exist at the time when the application is made, the procedure is comparatively simple.

The landlord applies to the local authority for a qualification certificate. The local authority before considering the application serves on the tenant a notice giving him an opportunity to raise objections within 28 days. If after considering the objections (if any) the local authority is satisfied that the certificate should be issued, they issue it; if not, they refuse it. Against the issue of the certificate the tenant, and against the refusal of the certificate the landlord, can appeal to the County Court within 28 days of receiving the certificate or notice of refusal.

In the second case, ie if the amenities do not yet exist, the landlord may apply for a provisional qualification certificate, specifying the works which he intends to carry out. Such an application may be made together with the application for a standard grant.

If the tenant objects to the carrying out of the works involved, the landlord may apply to the County Court for an order empowering the landlord to enter the premises and carry out the works.

The conditions of granting such an order are:

(a) that the works were specified in an application for a grant under Part I of the Housing Act 1969;

(b) that the works are specified in the certificate of provisional approval and that the local authority stated that the dwelling would satisfy the qualifying conditions when the works have been carried out.

In addition to these statutory conditions, which must be satisfied if the Court decides to issue the order sought, the Court, in determining whether the order should be made, shall have regard to all the circumstances, and in particular to:

(a) any disadvantage to the tenant, which may be expected to result from the work (eg the internal arrangements of rooms may be less convenient for the requirements of the tenant);

(b) the accommodation that might be available for him whilst the works are carried out;

(c) the age and health of the tenant.

The Court, however, shall not take into account the means or resources of the tenant (as it had to under the 1969 Act) in view of the fact that the allowance now paid by the local authority is supposed to help the tenant if his means are insufficient to pay the increased rent.

Once the local authority has issued a provisional qualification certificate the landlord can apply to the Rent Officer for a certificate of fair rent (see § 64). After the works have been completed and after the local authority has issued the final qualification certificate, the landlord may apply within three months to the Rent Officer for registration of the fair rent.

Immediately on the issue of the qualification certificate the tenancy ceases to be a controlled tenancy and becomes a regulated one. The increase of the rent from controlled into regulated is phased: the rent may be increased by one third immediately, by a further third after the first year and by the last third after the second year. The increase, however, may amount to 50 pence per week each year, even if it means a shortening of the period of phasing, which is usually two years.

75 Conversion of Controlled Tenancies into Regulated. General Decontrol

Section 35 of the Housing Finance Act 1972 provides that all controlled tenancies should become regulated tenancies on the dates specified in Subsection 2. The date of decontrol depends on the rateable value of the premises on 31 March 1972.

Table

Dwelling house in Greater London	Dwelling House elsewhere	
Rateable value on 31 March 1972	Rateable value on 31 March 1972	Date of conversion
£95 or more	£60 or more	1 January 1973
£80 – £95	£45 – £60	1 July 1973
£70 – £80	£35 – £45	1 January 1974
£60 – £70	£25 – £35	1 July 1974
£50 – £60	£20 – £25	1 January 1975
less than £50	less than £20	1 July 1975

The Secretary of State for the Environment issued two Statutory Instruments:

– Counter Inflation (Rents) (England and Wales) Order 1972 S.I. 1851/1972 and
– Counter Inflation (Rents) (England and Wales) Order 1973 S.I. 269/1973 postponing the first date of the conversion, ie 1 January 1973 to 29 April 1973.

Two further Statutory Instruments:

(a) Regulated Tenancies (Conversion from Control) Order 1973 S.I.752, and

(b) Regulated Tenancies (Conversion from Control) Order 1974 S.I.615

postponed the general conversion of all those tenancies which were due to be converted before 1 January 1975 until that date.

Section 36 excludes from general decontrol houses which have been condemned by the local authority as unfit for human habitation not later than three months before the date of conversion, but even then, if the landlord repairs the house to such an extent that it is made fit, the conversion takes place.

After the tenancy has been converted into a regulated one, the parties may reach agreement as to the amount of rent to be paid. Such agreements may be made on or after 1 January 1973. There is, however, one requirement in respect of these agreements: the landlord has to give the local authority a document in a prescribed form showing the particulars of the agreement and statements:

(a) that the tenant's security of tenure will not be affected if he refuses to enter into the agreement;

(b) that the tenant is not deprived of the right to refer the case to the Rent Officer for determination and registration of the fair rent.

A copy of the document should be sent to the tenant (Section 44 (5)) of the Housing Finance Act 1972.

Schedule 6 to the Housing Finance Act 1972 provides that on the first registration of a fair rent after the conversion of a controlled tenancy into a regulated one under Section 35 (general decontrol) an increase of rent may be recovered only in stages, the usual period being two years. The same staging is applied if the parties agree the amount of rent, as explained above.

Chapter 19

FURNISHED LETTINGS*

76 Limitation of Rent

Until the Rent Act 1968. which consolidated the provisions in respect of protection of dwelling houses, the Rent Acts did not apply to a dwelling house let bona fide at a rent which included payments for board, attendance or use of furniture, provided that the amount of rent attributable to the attendance or the use of furniture formed a substantial portion of the whole rent.

In the case of Palser v Grinling (1946) the Court Appeal expressed the view that 20% of the whole rent would be a substantial portion, but on appeal the House of Lords refused to lay down a hard and fast rule. In the case of Goel v Sagoo (1969) it was stated: 'in deciding what proportion of the total rent is fairly attributable to attendance or the use of furniture, the Court must be guided by common sense consideration rather than by any formula; the cost for the landlord is a relevant factor, though the primary factor is the value to the tenant'.

Until the end of the Second World War it was not considered necessary to protect furnished tenancies, but the acute shortage of any kind of accommodation after the war necessitated the enactment of a law protecting even those tenancies. The Furnished Houses (Rent Control) Act 1946 was originally intended to continue in force until the end of 1947 only, but it was extended and, with some amendments. is now included in the Rent Act 1968 (Part VI).

The Act applied to all contracts relating to dwellings whose rateable value did not exceed (on 23 March 1965) £400 in Greater London and £200 elsewhere. Under the Landlord and Tenant Act, the Furnished Lettings (Rateable Value Limits) Order 1973 S.I.869 (issued under Section 89 of the Housing Finance Act 1972, as amended by Sections 14(3) and 23(3) of, and a Schedule 6 to the Counter Inflation Act 1973) which came into operation on 1 June 1973, the rateable value of dwellings first entered in the valuation

96

*See Appendix A — Summary of Rent Act 1974

list on or after 1 April 1973 has been increased for Greater London to £1000, for the rest of the country to £500. This change is, of course, the result of re-valuation of hereditaments with effect from 1 April 1973.

The protection afforded by Part VI of the Rent Act 1968 does not apply to boarding houses or houses let for holidays.

If a tenant of a furnished dwelling considers that the rent paid by him is excessive, he can complain to the Rent Tribunal. The Rent Tribunals have been set up in Boroughs or Urban or District Councils and in London Boroughs.

The Rent Tribunals, whose jurisdiction is limited to furnished accommodation, should not be confused with the Rent Assessment Committees, whose jurisdiction applies to regulated tenancies. It is inconvenient that two separate tribunals have been constituted to deal with these two types of tenancies. The Francis Committee suggested their amalgamation, but this recommendation has not been accepted by the Government. In practice, however, the same persons serve on both tribunals; they meet on different days, sometimes as a 'Rent Tribunal' and sometimes as a 'Rent Assessment Committee'.

Both jurisdictions are, however, strictly separated and in the case of Goel v Sagoo (1969) the High Court made a quite understandable statement when it said that it is not proper for a tenant to apply to the Rent Tribunal in respect of a furnished tenancy and, after obtaining a reduction of rent, to apply to the Court for the protection of his tenancy as if it were an unfurnished one.

The Rent Tribunal, after making necessary enquiries and after giving both parties an opportunity to be heard, can either approve the rent or reduce it. Only exceptionally may the rent be increased if it includes cost of services or rates and those costs increase in value. · The local authority, after being notified about the assessment of rent, registers it in a special register of furnished lettings (different from that register in respect of regulated tenancies) and the registered rent can only be charged for the accommodation, unless there is a change in circumstances.

Thus the landlord cannot obtain an increase in the contractual or registered rent (unless there is an increase in the cost of services or rates borne by him) and this provision, which theoretically has frozen rents for furnished accommodation (if registered) since 1946 is somewhat unrealistic. It is a known fact that landlords after making a very small change in the furniture provided, claim 'change of circumstances' and increase the rent. This, to be fair, is quite reasonable in view of the rate of inflation.

Allowances in respect of rent for unfurnished lettings, introduced by the Housing Finance Act 1972 were extended to furnished tenancies by Furnished Lettings (Rent Allowances) Act 1973. Local authorities have the right to refer cases of furnished tenancies to the Rent Tribunals in order to obtain a reduction of rent if it is considered excessive.

77 Furnished Tenancies, Security of Tenure

Security of tenure is given solely by deferring the effect of notices to quit and for this reason it does not apply to fixed term tenancies. As these are terminated without the necessity of giving a notice to quit, they do not enjoy any security of tenure under Part VI of the Act. But even in these tenancies eviction may be effected only by obtaining a court order and the tenant has the right to ask for relief within the limits described in Chapter 20.

With regard to security of tenure in periodic tenancies of furnished accommodation, the provisions apply in two separate circumstances (Sections 77 – 80):

(a) where the notice to quit is given by the landlord after there has been a reference to a Rent Tribunal by the tenant;

(b) where a notice to quit is given by the landlord and the tenant afterwards (but before the notice expires) applies to the Rent Tribunal for a security of tenure.

A landlord's notice to quit given after a reference to the Rent Tribunal does not take effect until the end of six months since the reference. The delay is automatic and does not need a specific decision of the Tribunal to be brought into effect. However, the Tribunal has power to direct that the delay shall be for a period shorter than six months in the circumstances given below and with the consequences pointed out.

The second situation is, where the landlord serves a notice to quit before there has been a reference to the Tribunal by the tenant. In such a case the tenant can refer the case to the Tribunal before the expiry of the notice to quit. The Tribunal can then defer the date on which the notice to quit will have effect for any period up to six months. This delay, however, is not automatic: it must be applied for, and the delay is granted by the Tribunal as a discretionary remedy.

Thus the jurisdiction of the Tribunal extends to granting security of tenure for a period up to six months only in the first instance. Before the expiration of the six months, however, the tenant may apply again for a further extension for an additional period of up to six months and so on. This right of application for an extension is possessed also by the tenant who enjoys an automatic extension granted in the case mentioned under (a) above.Therefore, in theory, it means that the tenant who performs his obligations may enjoy unlimited security, provided that he applies every six months for an extension. In practice, however, the Rent Tribunal is reluctant to grant more than one or two extensions; thus the security of tenure in furnished tenancies is rather limited.

If the tenant is entitled to six months' delay as a result of his security of tenure either under automatic delay (case (a)), or by the Tribunal using his discretion by granting six months security (case (b)), – the landlord may apply to the Tribunal with a request that the period of security of tenure be reduced on certain grounds, namely:

(a) that the tenant has not complied with the terms of the contract;

(b) that the tenant (or a member of his household) has caused a nuisance or annoyance to neighbours or has been convicted of using the dwelling for immoral or illegal purposes;

(c) that due to the tenant's conduct the condition of the dwelling has deteriorated.

If the Rent Tribunal directs a shortening of the six months' period, the tenant cannot apply for a further extension of the security of tenure.

Note:

The Rent Bill 1974 proposes several important amendments of Part VI of the Rent Act which afford greater protection to furnished tenancies.

The Bill provides that furnished tenancies will become protected tenancies, thus enjoying the same protection as unfurnished ones.

The following tenancies, however, are excluded from such protection:

(a) tenancies where the landlord lives in the same building as the tenant, even if the tenant lives in a self-contained flat;

(b) tenancies occupied by students of specified educational

institutions;

(c) lettings for holiday seasons.

Schedule III of the 1968 Act (grounds for obtaining possession by landlords) is changed in respect of furnished tenancies. A new ground for possession (case 3a) is added, namely, if the tenant illtreats furniture. Another ground is added as case 10B, namely the letting of out-of-season holiday accommodation. Such a letting must be for a period not exceeding 8 months; the landlord must give a suitable notice at the beginning of the tenancy and the premises have to have been used for holiday lettings within the previous 12 months.

The protection of the furnished lettings excluded from the provisions of the Rent Bill 1974 remains unchanged, ie as enacted by the Part VI of the 1968 Rent Act. The following amendments, however, are being made to the Rent Act 1968:

(a) A Rent Tribunal may increase the contractual rent; until now only reduction of rent was possible unless there had been a change of circumstances;

(b) Rent may be reviewed by a Rent Tribunal every three years.*

*The bill, without any significant amendments, has been passed by Parliament and came into operation on 14 August 1974.

Chapter 20

PROTECTED TENANCIES. ANCILLARY PROVISIONS

Note: Some of these ancillary provisions apply not only to protected and statutory tenancies, but also to the tenancies of dwelling houses outside the provisions of the Rent Act.

78 Unlawful Eviction and Harassment of Occupiers
Section 30 of the Rent Act 1965 (not repealed by the Rent Act 1968) created two statutory criminal offences:

(a) the unlawful deprivation of the residential occupier (ie even a licensee) of any premises, unless the accused proved that he had reasonable cause to believe that the residential occupier had ceased to reside in the premises;

(b) the doing of acts calculated to interfere with the peace or comfort of the residential occupier or members of his household, or persistently withdrawing or withholding services reasonably required for the occupation of the premises as a residence.

These offences are tried summarily and are punishable by a fine and/or imprisonment.

79 Rent Books
Under the Landlord and Tenant Act 1962 (Section 1 and 4) it is provided that a rent book must be given to any residential tenant if the rent is payable weekly. The rent book must contain the provisions of the Housing Act 1957 relating to overcrowding, and other information about the protection of tenancies under the Rent Act 1968. It is a criminal offence (punishable by a fine) for the landlord to fail to comply with these provisions.

80 Restrictions on Premiums
It is also a criminal offence under Section 85 (of the Rent Act 1968) to require or receive a payment of any premium as a condition of the grant, renewal or continuance of a tenancy

protected by the Act, whether furnished or unfurnished. Where the purchase of any furniture, fittings or other articles is required as a condition of the grant, renewal, continuance or assignment of a tenancy subject to the Act, and the price exceeds the reasonable price of those articles, the excess is to be treated as a premium.

81 Restriction on Levying Distress for Rent

As has been mentioned in §55, no distress of rent of any dwelling house to which the Rent Act 1968 applies may be levied without the leave of the County Court (Section 111). Upon such application the Court has the power of adjournment, stay, suspension, or postponement of the distress as it may consider reasonable in the circumstances.

82 Prohibition of Eviction without Due Process of Law

Under Sections 31 and 32 of the Rent Act 1965 (not repealed by the 1968 Rent Act), where any premises have been let as a dwelling (whether protected by the Rent Act or not) it is not lawful to enforce the right of entry otherwise than by proceedings in the Court.

The Court during such proceedings may give similar relief to the tenant as on an application for leave to levy distress (see also § 49).

83 Shared Accommodation

The full protection of the Rent Act is given only to accommodation let as a separate dwelling (Section 1 (1)). If accommodation is shared, only a limited protection is afforded by Section 101 and 102.

It is not easy to decide what degree of sharing deprives the accommodation of the status of a 'separate dwelling', but some Court decisions are helpful.

Thus the sharing of the hall, bathroom and WC does not deprive the dwelling of its character as a separate dwelling (Cole v Harris 1945), but the sharing of the bathroom, WC and kitchen makes the accommodation 'shared' and not separate (Llewellyn v Hinson 1948). If , however, the kitchen is shared for the limited purpose of washing, but not cooking, the dwelling is a separate one (Goodrich v Paisner 1956).

There are two types of sharing. The accommodation may be shared with the landlord, or with other tenants. The two types are treated differently by Sections 101 and 102 respectively.

If a tenant has exclusive occupation of any accommodation and, in addition, shares other accommodation with his landlord, or with his landlord and other persons, he is entitled to protection as if he occupied furnished accommodation, even if no furniture is provided.

If a tenant shares some living accommodation with persons other than the landlord, the separate accommodation, which is used by the tenant exclusively is protected in the normal way as appropriate (ie either as protected or statutory tenancy, being either controlled or regulated).

84 Jurisdiction

The County Court has exclusive jurisdiction in the four following matters;

(a) as to whether a tenancy is a protected tenancy, or whether any person is a statutory tenant;

(b) as to the rent limit (in controlled tenancies);

(c) as to the rent actually recoverable under a controlled tenancy;

(d) as to the application of Part VI (dealing with furnished tenancies) to a contract.

Other problems are within the County Court jurisdiction if the rateable value of the premises do not exceed £400.

Chapter 21

LONG TENANCIES

85 Landlord and Tenant Act 1954 Part I

The Rent Acts have never applied to tenancies under which the tenant pays a rent which is less than two-thirds of the rateable value of the house and they still do not apply to such tenancies. This provision (based on the contemporary rateable value) applies to all tenancies with one exception: if after the conversion of controlled into regulated tenancies under the 1972 Housing Finance Act the rent (possibly in view of re-valuation on 1 April 1973) falls below two-thirds of the rateable value, the tenancy will, nevertheless, be protected.

Thus, if the rent is under two-thirds of the rateable value, the tenant has no protection when his contractual tenancy ends, unless the tenancy is for a term exceeding 21 years, when Part I of the 1954 Act applies. As practically all low rent tenancies consist of building leases, under which the tenant pays a large initial amount and afterwards a ground rent only (which is invariably under two-thirds of the rateable value), we may accept that virtually all long tenancies fall outside the Rent Act 1968, but under the 1954 Landlord and Tenant Act.

A tenancy, in order to be protected by Part I of the 1954 Landlord and Tenant Act, must be a long tenancy (over 21 years) at low rent (under two-thirds of the rateable value) and the rateable value should be within the limits imposed by the 1968 Rent Act. In addition the tenancy must be such as it would be within the Rent Act if the tenancy had not been at a low rent (ie it must be a separate dwelling, the house must not be under a furnished letting and the landlord must not belong to certain public bodies set out in Section 5 of the Rent Act 1968). Putting it in a nutshell we may say that the Act covers long tenancies at a low rent to which the Rent Act 1968 would apply if the rent were not low.

There are elaborate procedural requirements as to the creation of a statutory tenancy after the contractual tenancy has been terminated. There is an important condition that the property has to be let as a dwelling house and that the tenant has to occupy it as his residence.

The security of tenure given by the Act is very similar to the security afforded by the Rent Act 1968 (see § 68). There is one additional ground for terminating the tenancy, namely if the landlord intends to demolish or reconstruct the premises for purposes of re-development. On the other hand, three grounds of asking for possession are not included in the 1954 Act:

(a) the tenant has given notice to quit and, in consequence, the landlord has contracted to sell or let the premises;

(b) the tenant, without the consent of the landlord has at any time after the commencement of the Rent Act assigned or sub-let the whole dwelling house;

(c) the dwelling house is reasonably required by the landlord for himself or members of his family.

With regard to the rent which the tenant will have to pay after the termination of the contractual, long tenancy, the procedure for the determination of the fair rent under the Rent Act 1968 applies. The rent is determined and registered by the Rent Officer with the right of referring the case to the Rent Assessment Committee if the tenant or landlord is not satisfied with the Rent Officer's determination (Section 39 of the Leasehold Reform Act 1967).

The provisions of the 1954 Landlord and Tenant Act referring to long tenancies had their important applications for some 13 years, until the 1967 Leasehold Reform Act was enacted which allows certain leaseholders either to acquire their freehold or to obtain an extension of their existing lease for an additional 50 years.

86 Leasehold Reform Act 1967. Stating the Problem

Note: In paragraphs 78 − 83 all statutory references are references to the Leasehold Reform Act 1967 unless otherwise stated.

The Leasehold Reform Act 1967 was preceded by the White Paper 'Leasehold Reform in England and Wales' (Cmnd 2916), which explained the problem of leasehold reform. The White Paper stated that experience had shown that the system of long leases had worked very unfairly against the occupying leaseholder. It was considered indefensible that at the end of the term the law should allow the ownership of the house to revert to the freeholder, who got not only the land but also the house, the improvements and everything else the leaseholder and his predecessor had added to it. In the Government's view, the occupying leaseholder was morally entitled to the ownership of the building and the freeholder to the ownership of the land only.

Although the main principle of this legislation seem to be simple enough, the Act in its detailed provisions creates many complex problems and here it is intended only to summarise the provisions of the Act. A judge of the Court of Appeal in Central Estates (Belgravia) Ltd v Woolgar (1971) stated: 'It is an ill-designed piece of legislation, which has caused endless litigation. It was designed to help deserving tenants, where the leaseholder had in effect been paid the value of the house over and over again'. (The case concerned a tenant who was convicted for keeping a brothel and, in order to avoid forfeiture of the lease, submitted a claim for enfranchisement. The Court accepted that the claim had not been made in good faith and granted leave to the landlord to bring forfeiture proceedings under Schedule 3, Paragraph 4(1), thus vitiating the claim for enfranchisement).

87 Leasehold Reform Act 1967. Qualifying Conditions

Sections 1–4 of the Act set the conditions which must be satisfied to give a tenant the right either to acquire the freehold ('enfranchisement') or to extend his lease ('extension'):

(a) the applicant must be the tenant of a leasehold house;

(b) the tenancy must be a long tenancy;

(c) the tenancy must be at a low rent;

(d) the rateable value of the house and premises on the appropriate day must not have been more than £400 in Greater London or £200 elsewhere; the 'appropriate day' means either 23 March 1965 or, if the house appeared for the first time in the valuation list after that date, the date of entry on the list.

(e) the tenant has to occupy the premises as his only or main residence either for the last five years or for periods amounting to five years in the last ten years;

(f) the house must not be:

(i) let to or occupied by the tenant with other land or premises to which it is ancillary; or

(ii) comprised in an agricultural holding within the meaning of

106

the Agricultural Holdings Act 1948 (see § 99).
Some of the conditions require comments.

(a) House

The meaning of 'house' for the purposes of the Act is explained in Section 2. 'House' includes any building, designed or adapted for living in and reasonably so called, notwithstanding that the building is not structurally detached, or is not solely designed for living in. It must not, however, be divided horizontally into flats or maisonettes; and

(i) where a building is divided horizontally, the flats or other units into which it is so divided are not separate 'houses', though the building as a whole may be;

(ii) where a building is divided vertically, the building as a whole is not a 'house', though any of the units into which it is divided may be.

A 'house' does not include a building which is not structurally detached and of which a material part lies above or below a part of the structure not comprised in the house. Thus this definition of a "house" includes semi-detached houses, but not flats or maisonettes. Any garage, outhouse, garden, yard and appurtenances let with the house are included in the definition.

The question of what building is 'reasonably called a house' creates some problems. The statutory definitions in many pre-1967 Acts do not help much. So far there have been only a few cases in which the Court has had to consider the meaning of 'house' under the Leasehold Reform Act. In the case Lake v Bennett (1969) a leasehold property was built as a house some 100 years ago. The ground floor was let off (or, strictly speaking, sub-let off) as a licensed betting shop and the tenant lived in the upper floors and basement. The building was accepted as a 'house' for the purpose of the Leasehold Reform Act. In Harris v Swick Securities Ltd (1969) it was held that if a person occupied a part of the house himself and sublet part of the house to four families, he still occupied the house in part and was entitled to take advantage of the Act.

Subsection 4–7 of the Section 2 gives the landlord the right to exclude from the enfranchisement mines and minerals after ensuring proper support to the structure of the house. The landlord has also some rights to include in the premises or exclude from the premises some land which it is reasonable to include or to exclude from enfranchisement. If there is a dispute on this matter the Court

107

decides the issue.

(b) Long tenancy (Section 3)

A long tenancy is a tenancy granted for a term exceeding 21 years.

Two special cases are included in the definition of 'long tenancy':

(i) a tenancy contracted for a term exceeding 21 years remains in the scope of the Act, even if it is terminable before the end of its term by a notice of the landlord to the tenant;

(ii) a tenancy for a term not exceeding 21 years with a covenant for renewal without payment of a premium and if there has been one or more renewals so that the total of the term now exceeds 21 years.

Any period during which the tenancy continues under Part I or Part II of the Landlord and Tenant Act 1954 is included in a long tenancy.

However, the agreement cannot antedate the date from which the lease has started. Thus in Roberts v Church Commissioners (1971) on 15 May 1950 the tenant signed a contract for the grant to him of a lease of certain premises for a term of 10¼ years from 25 May 1950. In June 1952 it was agreed that the lease should be extended to June 1971. The lease was dated 29 October 1952 and by it the premises were demised for a term of 21¼ years from 1 September 1950. It was held that this lease was not a 'long tenancy', as at no time during the tenancy did the tenant actually had a term for 21 years.

(c) Low Rent (Section 4).

Low rent means a rent which amounts to less than two-thirds of the rateable value on the 'appropriate day'.

The appropriate day is the latest of the three following dates:

(i) 23 March 1965;

(ii) the date on which the premises first appeared in the valuation list;

(iii) the first day of the lease.

The exception is made for tenancies (other than building leases) which were granted between the end of August 1939 and beginning of April 1963; these leases must have been under two-thirds of the *rateable value* at the beginning of the tenancy even although this date falls before 23 March 1965. Thus pre-war tenancies may be accepted as at a low rent, although at their creation the rent might have exceeded the limit, but this does not apply to tenancies created between the beginning of the Second World War and April 1963.

(d) Rateable Value

In deciding whether the house fulfils this condition an interesting problem arises when two houses are converted into one residence. Two cases explain the Court's attitude:

In Peck v Anicar Properties Ltd (1971) the tenant held a long lease at a low rent of a building comprising a shop on the ground floor and residential accommodation above, where he lived. A staircase connected the shop with the dwelling accommodation. Entrances to the shop and to the dwelling accommodation were from different roads. The tenant was also lessee under a separate agreement of the next door building which likewise was a shop with dwelling accommodation above. A hole had been made in the wall between the two shops, which were used by the tenant as one. There was no communication between the dwelling accommodation in the two buildings and the dwelling accommodation in the next door building was let by the tenant to someone else. The tenant applied to acquire the freehold of the building where he lived. It was held by the Court of Appeal that a mere hole knocked through into the next building did not affect the fact that the building where the tenant lived was a separate building and might be enfranchised.

Wolf v Crutchley and Another (1971) concerned two adjoining terrace houses let by the defendant to the plaintiff. Each house taken separately was within the rateable value limits, but taken together exceeded £400 for Greater London, where the premises were situated. The plaintiff had taken steps to use the two houses together and made an opening on the first floor of the houses from one to the other. Since that time the plaintiff had used the two houses together and taken in girl students from a nearby ballet academy. Living herself in one of the houses, the plaintiff claimed to be entitled to enfranchise it. The defendant claimed that the two houses had become one and were outside the rateable value limit. The Court of Appeal decided that the house where the plaintiff lived was a separate house and the connecting door had not deprived the house of this character.

(e) Only or Main Residence (Section 1 (2) 2)

In Fowell v Radford (1970) Lord Denning said: 'While it was unusual there is nothing to prevent each spouse having his own main residence for the purposes of the Leasehold Reform Act 1967. This is a question of fact'.

With respect to the 5 years requirement under Section 7, where the tenant of a house dies while occupying it as his residence, a member of his family resident in the house becomes tenant under the same tenancy and (provided that he satisfies the requirement as to residence) may apply for enfranchisement or extension of the lease. A member of the deceased family is widely defined and the definition includes: spouse, children and parents (and the parents and children include mother- and father-in-law and son- and daughter-in-law).

Under Section 5 a tenant who has given a notice to the landlord claiming enfranchisement or extension can assign the tenancy with the benefit of the existing notice; if he assigns without the benefit of the notice, the notice ceases to have any effect and the assignee (the new tenant) has to fulfil the conditions in his own rights.

88 Leasehold Reform Act 1967. Enfranchisement (Sections 8 - 13)

Where a tenant of a house fulfils the qualifying conditions discussed in § 87 he has a right to acquire the freehold of the house, free from encumbrances.

The price of the freehold may be agreed between the parties; if no agreement can be reached, it is the Lands Tribunal who assesses the price. The price is assessed on the assumption that the landlord's interest is restricted to the land and that the house ('bricks and mortar') belongs to the occupying tenant. In order to achieve this the Act provides that the price is to be the amount which would be realised on the open market on the assumption that the vendor was selling the freehold subject to the existing tenancy and that the tenancy, if not already extended, was to be extended for 50 years.

The first case decided by the Lands Tribunal (Custin v Heart of Oak Benevolent Society 1969) assessed the price of the freehold higher than had been generally expected and it became clear that the interpretation of the Act as it stood defeated the intention of the legislature. For this reason the Housing Act 1969 added an amendment (Section 82) to the effect that the sitting tenant and members of his family should not be considered as potential purchasers.

Various methods of valuation have been adopted by valuers in submitting their evidence to the Lands Tribunal. Discussion of them is outside the scope of the book. It is intersting to note, however that in recent cases (Jenkins v Bevan Thomas 1972, 221 *Estates Gazette* 640, Barber v Trustees of Eltham United Charities 1972, 221 *Estates Gazette* 1343) if the unexpired lease amounted to 75 years, the Lands Tribunal assessed the price as an amount equivalent to ten times the ground rent. This simple method is used if the unexpired term amounts to about or over 75 years. The amount of compensation increases sharply the shorter the outstanding period of the lease becomes.

The tenant has a right to withdraw from the transaction when he has ascertained the amount to be payable, or likely to be payable. In such case he has to pay the landlord's costs and cannot again claim his right to enfranchisement for five years.

The conveyance is not framed in such a manner as to exclude or restrict the general words implied in conveyances under the Law of Property Act 1925. Generally speaking the tenant acquires the freehold burdened by the existing easements and restrictive covenants. Section 10 contains detailed provisions giving the landlord the right to create a new easement or restrictive covenant which are required by him as a result of dividing his property (if this is the case); on the other hand the tenant acquires the freehold with benefits of easements and restrictive covenants which are required by him after severance of the property acquired by him.

89 Leasehold Reform Act 1967. Extension (Sections 14 - 16)

If a tenant, fulfilling the qualifying conditions, gives to the landlord a written notice of his desire to have the lease extended, the landlord is bound to grant to the tenant a new lease for a term expiring 50 years after the existing tenancy. Thus, if the tenant having, say, 20 years of his existing lease to run, seeks to exercise his right to extension, the existing lease is terminated immediately and a new lease is granted forthwith for 70 years.

The landlord's costs connected with the granting of the new lease have to be borne by the tenant, who also has to clear arrears of rent (if any).

Generally speaking, the new tenancy is on the same terms as the old one, with any necessary adjustment due to change of circumstances (eg in case of exclusion from the new tenancy of a part of the property).

The rent for the remaining period of the contractual tenancy remains unchanged, but for the extended period it is a 'modern' rent, assessed in the last 12 months of the contractual tenancy (as only then the modern ground rent can be ascertained due to fluctuation of the value of money). The rent is a ground rent representing the value of the site (without building which, according to the philosophy of the Act, belongs to the tenant). This rent may be revised after 25 years on the request of the landlord expressed not earlier than 12 months before the expiration of the first 25 years of extension.

Until the termination date of the original tenancy arrives, the tenant can change his mind and ask for enfranchisement instead of extension of the lease. Once, however, the extension starts, the tenant cannot ask for enfranchisement. He has no further right to extension after the expiration of the 50 years provided by the Act, and he is not protected by Part I or II of the Landlord and Tenant Act 1954 (85) or even by the Rent Act 1968.

90 Leasehold Reform Act. Procedure and Jurisdiction

A tenant wishing to take advantage of the right to enfranchise or to extend the lease, has to give notice to the landlord on a form prescribed by Regulations (The Leasehold Reform (Notices) Regulations 1967 S.I.No 1768 as amended by S.I.1969 No.1481) provided, of course, that he qualifies under the conditions explained in § 87. There is a separate form of notice for acquiring a freehold and for demanding an extension of the lease. The Landlord should give within two months a counter-notice in the prescribed form stating whether he admits the tenant's right and if not, on what grounds he objects. Otherwise, if the landlord does not reply, it is assumed that the landlord does not object to the enfranchisement or extension, as the case may be.

Sections 20 and 21 deal with jurisdiction in dealing with disputes arising under the Act.

The County Court has jurisdiction in determining legal problems: whether a person is entitled to enfranchisement or extension, what provisions ought to be contained in the conveyance or in the lease and generally speaking other legal questions which may arise.

The Lands Tribunal whose jurisdiction on some points overlaps with that of the County Court, is responsible for determination of the price payable for the freehold of the house, for determination of the rent during the extended lease and for assessment of compensation payable to the tenant under Section 17 or 18

112

of the Act (see § 91).

Overlapping jurisdiction exists in respect of provisions which ought to be introduced in a conveyance or lease, apportionment of rent if premises are split, etc. There are provisions for the County Court to transfer cases to the Lands Tribunal in a case of overlapping jurisdiction should it be considered convenient.

91 Leasehold Reform Act. Landlord's Rights Overriding the Tenant's Claims for Enfranchisement or Extension

Sections 17 − 19 deal with those rights of the landlord which take priority over the tenant's claims.

Section 17 applies only to cases where the extension has been granted and not to enfranchisement. Under this Section the landlord is empowered to apply to the County Court at any time during the extended period, or within 12 months before it begins, for an order granting possession of the premises to him for purposes of redevelopment; and the Court on being satisfied that the landlord has established his grounds, must make a declaratory order that he is entitled to possession. The tenant is entitled to compensation for the loss of the house and premises, which (as stated in Schedule 2 § 5) amount to the price of the leasehold of the house and the premises if sold in the open market by a willing seller under the assumption that the lease has been extended for 50 years.

Section 18 applies to the cases of both enfranchisement and extension. When the tenant has given notice that he intends to excercise his right of enfranchisement or extension, the landlord may, at any time before effect is given to the notice (which probably means at any time before the freehold is conveyed or the new lease granted to the tenant), apply to the Court for possession of the property. The landlord has to fulfil certain conditions, the most important being:

(a) that he requires to occupy the premises as the only or main residence of himself or a member of his family;

(b) that the landlord's interest has been created or purchased before 18 February 1966 (this date has been chosen because it is the date on which the White Paper on Leasehold Reform was published); this means that the landlord had to acquire the interest in full expectation that the long lease would terminate at the end of the contractual term (subject to tenant's rights under Landlord and Tenant Act 1954);

(c) a 'greater hardship' proviso (similar to that under the Rent Act 1968 – § 68 (h)) is to be applied by the Court.

Under Section 2 of Schedule 2 the tenancy shall determine (and compensation becomes payable) on a date fixed by the Court, which cannot be earlier than four months and not later than 12 months after the termination of the contractual tenancy.

Here again the tenant is entitled to compensation assessed on similar lines to compensation under Section 17 explained above.

Section 19 ('Retention of Management Powers for General Benefit of Neighbourhood') allows the landlord to retain powers of management of any area which may be subject to enfranchisement in order to preserve the benefits which are at present enjoyed in well-managed estates (eg Dulwich Estate in London). The powers of the landlord, covenanted in the leases to ensure upkeep for the general good of the neighbourhood, would be lost on enfranchisement were not these special provisions included. This Section applies if there is an area which, at the commencement of the Act, was occupied directly or indirectly under tenancies held from one landlord. The landlord's application had to be made within two years after the commencement of the Act to the Secretary of State for the Environment. The Secretary, after considering the reasonableness of the application, may issue a certificate allowing the landlord to retain powers of management after enfranchisement. These powers should be clearly defined in the 'Scheme of Management' attached to the application. As the Scheme limits the rights of the fee simple owners (ie the tenants after the enfranchisements), such a certificate must be approved by the High Court and is registered under the Land Charges Act 1925 as a local land charge and will be enforceable as a restrictive covenant. However, it may go further than a restrictive covenant, as it may be active in its content, imposing on the tenants – future freeholders – various positive duties, including payments of contributions towards the upkeep of the area covered by the scheme. The landlord of the Management Scheme may assign his rights and powers to somebody else (eg a local authority or association of owners).

Section 28 deprives the tenant of his right to enfranchisement or extension, where the landlord is a local authority or some other public body (eg Commission for New Town, or Universities, Regional Hospital Boards, National Industries, Port Authorities, etc) and the appropriate Minister certifies that the property will be required for relevant development within the next ten years.

Chapter 22

BUSINESS TENANCIES

92 Business Tenancies. Introduction

Being the least controversial of all branches of social legislation, the law of business tenancies is perhaps therefore that which has produced the best results. It has remained to a large extent outside politics, as it has been generally acknowledged that some kind of statutory protection of tenants of business premises is necessary, for otherwise there would be a possibility of hardship to the tenants in the following circumstances, pointed out by Adkin in his book *Landlord and Tenant:*

(a) tenants of business premises have, in some cases, expended large sums of money upon making improvements, but, on the determination of their contractual tenancies the benefit of such improvements has passed to their landlords, who have been able to obtain an increased rent.

(b) tenants may have agreed not to alter the premises without the consent of their landlord and the consent may be unreasonably refused;

(c) tenants may, in the course of years, build up a good trade in connection with certain premises and at the end of the lease the landlord may ask for a greatly increased rent owing to the goodwill attached to the premises.

Thus, it may be seen that whereas in tenancies of dwelling houses the two problems are security of tenure and limitation of rent, in business tenancies limitation of rent to a reasonable amount is of some importance, but the main problems are security of tenure and compensation for improvements.

These two aspects are the concern not only of the tenant, but also of the community at large, which is interested in having as modern and efficient business establishments as possible. Tenants must be induced to modernise their premises, which they will do if they are, at least to some extent, sure that the tenancy will not be

116

inequitably terminated. Also, the tenant will be induced to modernise the premises only if, provided that the improvements are reasonable, he will be able to expect compensation for the money spent on the termination of the tenancy.

Until 1927 there was a completely free market in respect of business premises, and it was only in that year that the Landlord and Tenant Act was passed, which provided in Part I for payment of compensation for improvement and for goodwill to tenants of business premises on termination of the tenancy. The provisions of the 1927 Act never worked properly in relation to compensation for loss of goodwill and these provisions were, eventually, replaced by more comprehensive protection in the Landlord and Tenant Act 1954, which in Part II deals with business tenancies.

15 years after the passing of the 1954 Act it appeared necessary to amend it considerably, mostly to plug some loopholes, which ingenious lawyers found in the Acts and used for avoidance of its provisions. These amendments have been introduced in the Law of Property Act 1969 (Sections 1 − 15).

Thus there are now the following Acts dealing with business tenancies: the Landlord and Tenant Act 1927 in respect of compensation for improvements and the Landlord and Tenant Act 1954, Part II (as amended by the Law of Property Act 1969) in respect of security of tenure and limitation of rent.

93 Business Tenancies; Definitions and Exclusions from the Acts

There are small differences between the tenancies to which the 1927 and the 1954 Act apply. Section 17 of the 1927 Act provides that the Act applies to 'the holdings used wholly or partly for carrying on thereat any trade or business' (trade and business are not defined). The Section excludes, however:

(a) mining leases;

(b) agricultural holdings;

(c) holdings let to tenants as holders of an office, appointment or employment (if the contract in writing expresses the purpose for which the tenancy has been created);

(d) premises used for carrying on thereat any profession;

(e) premises where the tenant carries on the business of subletting residential flats, even if meals are provided by the landlord.

Section 23 of the Landlord and Tenant Act 1954, stating that this part of the Act applies to any tenancy where the property is occupied

117

for the purposes of a business, does not define 'business' but provides that it includes a trade, profession (there is a difference here between the 1927 and 1954 Acts) or employment and includes any activity carried on by a body of persons, whether corporate or incorporate. The wording is extensive and eliminates the need of distinguishing between the various kinds of activities, which may qualify for protection.

There is a number of cases explaining what is meant by 'business'. Thus the following activities have been accepted as a 'business': a school, a hospital for poor persons paying according to their means, the taking of lodgers or paying guests, subletting of premises in apartments (again a difference between the two Acts), a tennis club carried on by a society, and a 'home' where working girls are boarded without payment.

The following types of leases are excluded from the provisions of the 1954 Act (they are, broadly speaking, similar to exclusions from 1927 Act, but there are some differences):

(a) mining leases (for, it is submitted, it is reasonable to suppose that it is not intended that a tenant who obtains a lease allowing him to remove minerals, should have a right to renew his lease for an indefinite period);

(b) agricultural holdings (as they are protected under separate legislation explained in Chapter 23);

(c) tenancies granted by reason of an office or employment;

(d) 'on licence' premises (ie pubs); except premises where the sale of alcohol does not form a major part of business, eg restaurants, hotels or refreshment rooms at railway stations);

(e) tenancies excluded by Section 9(3) of the Rent Act 1968. The combined result of Section 9(3) of the Rent Act 1968 and Section 43(1)(c) of the Landlord and Tenant Act 1954, as amended by Schedule 15 to the Rent Act 1968 is, that where the premises are in part business and in part residential, they are protected by the Rent Act 1968 if they are controlled, but they are protected under the 1954 Act, as business premises, if they are regulated. Thus, when controlled tenancies are all converted into regulated tenancies, the Rent Act 1968 will not apply to those premises, and they will be within the protection of the 1954 Act.

(f) 'short tenancies'. Originally, under the 1954 Act, tenancies for a period not exceeding three months were excluded, but the Law of Property Act 1969 (Section 12) amended the 1954 Act.

118

Now a tenancy is exempted if it is for a term certain of not more than six months, provided that the tenant has not been in occupation for a period which exceeds 12 months (this period includes any period during which the predecessor in the carrying on of the business was in occupation). Protection of short tenancies after 12 months possession has been introduced to prevent the stratagem by which the landlord granted to a tenant a succession of short tenancies, thus, in practice, evading the provisions of the 1954 Act.

94 Business Tenancies: Compensation for Improvement
   The tenant is not entitled to compensation for improvements in the following circumstances:
(a) if he effected them before 25 March 1928 (this is the date when the 1927 Act came into operation); the reason for this exclusion is that the landlord might have agreed to some improvements before March 1928 not expecting to be compelled to compensate for them. If, now, such a duty were imposed on him, he would be suffering unexpected loss. The tenant is not injured in any way, as he made these improvements not expecting any compensation;
(b) if he made them before 1 October 1954 in pursuance of a statutory obligation. This exclusion, introduced by the 1927 Act, was removed by the 1954 Act, but only in respect of future improvements;
(c) if he completed them before 1 October 1954 and less than three years before the termination of the tenancy. Before the 1954 Act came into operation (and before a degree of security of tenure was afforded to tenants) it was considered improvident to allow the making of improvements in the last three years of the contractual tenancy. If the making of such improvements were allowed, not only would the tenant lack sufficient time to use and profit from this improvement, but also the landlord would be saddled both with improvements of a nature he might not approve and with the obligation to compensate for them. The situation has been, of course, radically changed, since now the tenant can expect a new tenancy after his contractual tenancy has ended.
(d) if he made them in carrying out a contractual obligation; it may be safely assumed that if the tenant accepted an obligation

119

to effect certain improvement detailed in the lease agreement, he obtained some concession (eg in respect of the amount of rent) for accepting this duty.

Apart from these cases the tenant is entitled to compensation, provided that he uses the proper procedure both in affecting the improvements and in claiming the compensation.

Neither the 1927 nor the 1954 Act defines what improvements entail. Improvements must fulfil conditions stated in the Act in order to be recognised as 'proper improvements', ie improvements for which compensation may be claimed; 'proper improvements' will be explained later. Section 1 of the 1927 Act includes in improvements the erection of any building and those fixtures which the tenant has affixed but is not entitled to remove on the termination of the tenancy. Some Court's cases explain further what is understood by improvements. Thus the demolition of an existing building and the erection of a new one to be used for a new and different business may constitute an improvement (National Electric Theatres Ltd v Hudgell 1939).

In order to be able to claim compensation for intended improvement the tenant must serve on the landlord a notice of his intention to make the improvements with specifications and plans.

If the immediate landlord is himself a tenant, he should serve a copy of this notice to his superior landlord until the notice reaches the freeholder. The copies of all documents during the ensuing proceeding should be similarly served and in this case the immediate landlord, when his tenancy terminates, will be able to obtain compensation for improvements which he, in turn, paid to his tenant.

The immediate landlord has, on receipt of the notice, three courses of action open to him:

(a) he may offer to carry out the intended improvements himself. Such an offer must be accepted by the tenant and in this case the landlord is entitled to increase the rent as appropriate. The amount of the increase (if there is no agreement between the parties) will be determined by the Court;

(b) the landlord may reach an agreement with the tenant as to the work to be done by the tenant;

(c) the landlord may, within three months from receiving the notice, serve on the tenant a counter-notice, objecting to the tenant's intention. The tenant may then apply to the Court for a certificate that the improvements proposed by him are 'proper improvements'.

Improvements, in order to be recognised as 'proper improvements', have to possess the following features (Section 1(1) of the 1927 Act):

(a) they must be of such a nature as would on the termination of the tenancy add to the letting value of the holding. Thus the effect of the improvements must last beyond the time of the lease;

(b) they must be reasonable and suitable in view of the nature of the holding. This is a matter of fact for the Court to decide;

(c) they must not be such as would diminish the value of any other property belonging to the same landlord or to any superior landlord from whom the immediate landlord of the tenancy directly or indirectly holds.

If the certificate has been issued (either by the landlord on the request of the tenant or by the Court on the tenant's application), the tenant may make the improvements notwithstanding anything in the lease to the contrary.

When the work has been completed the tenant may require the landlord to give him a certificate that the improvements have been duly executed. If the landlord refuses to issue the certificate within one month from the demand, the tenant may apply to the Court for such a certificate. If the landlord issues the certificate when asked by the tenant, the latter has to pay the costs connected with the issue of the certificate (eg surveyor's fee). If the Court issues the certificate the costs are within the discretion of the Court.

If by reason of the executed improvements, rates or insurance premiums are increased, these additional amounts should be borne by the tenant, even if in the contract of lease it is the landlord who has been made responsible for these items.

When the tenant has completed the improvements, complied with the requirements described above and obtained the certificate, he acquires the right to claim compensation from his landlord on quitting the premises at the determination of the tenancy. He will be paid the compensation for improvements when he actually vacates the premises and not when his original tenancy ends and is extended by the Court.

When the end of the tenancy is approaching, the tenant must follow carefully the correct procedure in making the claim. The time of making the claim is now governed by Section 47 of the 1954 Act, which amended Section 1(1) of the 1927 Act:

(a) when the tenancy is about to end through the effluxion of time, the claim should be made not earlier than six, and not later than three months before its ending. This provision has only very exceptional application because, as it will be seen later (§ 87) business tenancies do not terminate by effluxion of time, but are automatically extended in ways described in the 1954 Act;

(b) when it is terminated by forfeiture or exercise of the right of entry, the claim should be made within three months from the Court order of forfeiture or within three months from re-entry which is effected without Court order;

(c) if the tenancy is terminated by a notice to quit, the period is three months from the date of such notice.

In the last case we face a difficulty. If a notice to quit is given by the tenant, it is clear that the tenancy will come to the end and service of claim for compensation should be arranged. If, however, the landlord serves the notice to quit and the tenant intends to object to it (as he is entitled in the situation described in the next paragraph), the problem arises whether the tenant should serve a claim for compensation (as he must do in order to obtain the compensation) and whether, should he do so, he is estopped from fighting the notice to quit? That the tenant was so estopped was argued by the landlords in two cases, but their argument was rejected. In Davis W. (Spitalfields) Ltd v Huntley (1947) it was stated: 'a tenant, when claiming compensation only is not bound to affirm that the notice is valid'. Similarly, and even more clearly, it was stated in Adler v Blackman (1952): 'claiming compensation by the tenant does not mean that he accepts the landlord's notice as a valid one'. Nevertheless in such a circumstance the safest course of action for the tenant is to claim compensation (as he has to do) but mention in the claim that it is done without prejudice to the validity of the notice to quit.

The landlord and tenant should try to reach an agreement in respect of the amount due for compensation. If no agreement can be reached, the Court decides the amount.

The sum paid as compensation is the lesser of the two following amounts (Section 1(1) of the 1927 Act):

(a) the net addition to the value of the holding as a whole which may be determined to be the direct result of the improvement at

122

the termination of the tenancy; or

(b) the reasonable cost or carrying out the improvements at the termination of the tenancy, after deducting the costs (if any) of putting the improvements into a reasonable state of repair.

The 'net' addition to the value signifies that if improvements diminish the value of the holding in some respects, such diminution should be set against the accretion in value (National Electric Theatres v Hudgell 1939).

In both amounts indicated above, the words 'at the termination of the tenancy' protect the tenant against devaluation of money spent some years previously by him on improvements.

In determining the amount of compensation regard should be paid to the landlord's intended use of the premises. If he intends to demolish them, the compensation may be reduced, or even completely refused, depending on the time between the termination of the tenancy and demolition.

95 Business Tenancies. Security of Tenure

The object of the 1954 Act is to give a general and automatic, but limited security of tenure to business tenancies which are within the scope of the Act. When the contractual tenancy ends, a statutory tenancy arises between the landlord and tenant, since the Act expressly states in Section 24(1) of the Act that: 'a tenancy to which this part of this Act applies shall not come to an end unless terminated in accordance with the provisions of this Part of the Act'.

Before discussing the methods by which business tenancies may be terminated a concept of 'competent landlord', ie the landlord for the purposes of the 1954 Act, should be explained. Section 44(1) states that the landlord for the purposes of the Act means not necessarily the immediate landlord, but the landlord (nearest to the tenant if there is a chain of tenancies and subtenancies) who holds either a reversion of at least 14 months' duration or the fee simple. Thus, if the reversion of the immediate landlord is only of, say, 9 months' duration, the tenant has to deal with the next superior landlord who fulfils this condition.

There are three possible methods of terminating tenancies of business premises:

(a) tenant's notice to terminate (Section 27);
(b) landlord's notice to terminate (Section 25);
(c) tenant's request for a new tenancy (Section 26).

(a) Tenant's notice to terminate

The tenancy ends if the tenant gives a notice to terminate it. A three months' notice is required either before the end of the tenancy which was contracted for a fixed term, or at any time if the tenancy is statutory, ie extended under the Act. If the tenancy is contractural, the tenant may give a valid notice according to the agreement. If the tenant terminates the lease in this manner, or surrenders the lease and the surrender is accepted by the landlord, he cannot take advantage of provisions of the Act giving him the right to ask for a new tenancy.

Section 4 of the 1969 Law of Property Act added a proviso that a notice to quit or an act of surrender by the tenant executed before the tenant has been in occupation of the premises for a period of one month is ineffective. This provision has been enacted in order to prevent the landlord obtaining surrender by the tenant (or obtaining a notice from the tenant) before the tenancy started, thus virtually evading the provisions of the 1954 Act.

(b) Landlord's notice to terminate

If the landlord gives notice to terminate (which should be given not more than 12 and not less than 6 months before the intended termination), he should indicate in the notice whether he requires the premises for himself, or is prepared to grant a new tenancy but is dissatisfied with the terms of the present tenancy and wants to change them. It is the tenant's duty to notify the landlord within two months whether he is willing to give up possession, or wants to continue the tenancy. Like the tenant, the landlord must not give the notice before the tenant has been in occupation of the tenancy for one month. If it were otherwise, the landlord might be tempted to give the tenant notice before the contract for tenancy was effected and the tenant may be compelled to accept the notice in order to obtain the tenancy. In such a manner the provisions of the Act would again be evaded.

Apart from the notice to terminate, the landlord may also forfeit the lease if the tenant commits a breach of a covenant. Here the general principles of the Law of Property Act 1925 apply and the tenant may ask for relief under Section 146 (see §57).

(c) Tenant's Request for a new tenancy

A request for a new tenancy may be made by the tenant where

the current tenancy is for a term certain exceeding one year, even if the term has expired and the tenancy has become a statutory tenancy.

It may seem superfluous to grant this right to the tenant if his tenancy does not terminate by effluxion of time and is automatically extended unless terminated in one of the methods discussed. The tenant will ask for a new tenancy if he intends to invest more money in his business and hence requires security lest his tenancy be terminated prematurely.

A tenant must request a tenancy beginning not more than 12 months and not less than 6 months from the date of the request. This is the same period (6 to 12 months) as is required for the landlord to give a notice to terminate the tenancy under (b) above. The request must be made in the prescribed form setting out the property to be let (which may be the whole or a part of the premises), the rent to be paid and the term of the new tenancy including its duration. In Bolsom (Sidney) Investment Trust Ltd v Karmios (E) & Co (London) Ltd (1956) it was accepted that if the tenant did not suggest the duration of the new tenancy, but requested a new tenancy 'upon the terms of the current tenancy', he proposed by implication a new tenancy of the same duration as the old one. The landlord has to notify the tenant of his objections to grant a new tenancy within two months, as otherwise it will be assumed (no relief being possible against this assumption), that the landlord agrees to the extension on the terms proposed by the tenant.

In the last two cases (b) and (c), ie where the landlord has given notice to terminate the tenancy and the tenant has duly served a counter-notice within two months as required by the Act, or where the tenant has asked for a new tenancy and the landlord within two months has objected to it, the tenant may at any time (being not less than two, but not more than four months after the notice to terminate the old tenancy, or the request for a new tenancy) apply to the Court for a new tenancy.

The Court must make an order granting a new tenancy unless the landlord successfully objects to such a grant on the grounds specified in the Act (Section 30(1)). The Court must be satisfied:

(a) that the tenant ought not to be granted a new tenancy, because he has failed to comply with his obligations to repair and maintain the premises; or

(b) that the tenant ought not to be granted a new tenancy in view of his persistent delay in paying rent which has become due; or

(c) that the tenant ought not to be granted a new tenancy in view of any other substantial breach of his obligations or for any other reason connected with the tenant's use or management of the premises; or

(d) that the landlord has offered and is willing to provide suitable alternative accommodation; or

(e) that if the tenancy is created by the subletting of part of the premises the superior landlord reasonably may expect to obtain a higher rent for letting the holding as a whole and he requires possession of the holding in order to let it in such a manner or otherwise dispose of it;

(f) that the landlord intends to demolish or reconstruct the holding and cannot reasonably do so without terminating the tenancy;

(g) that the landlord himself intends to carry on a business or live on the premises.

Point (f) was abused by some landlords who, intending to carry on minor developments used this ground as a pretext to terminate the tenancy. For this reason Section 7(1) of the Law of Property Act 1969 allows the Court to order the termination of the tenancy in respect of the part of the holding, if only a part is required by the landlord and the tenant is prepared to limit his holding to the part not required by the landlord.

If the creation of the new tenancy has been agreed between the parties, but they cannot agree its terms, the Court determines them. If the tenant finds that the terms determined by the Court are too onerous for him, he may, within 14 days, ask for the revocation of the Court Order granting the new tenancy on those terms, in which case the Court gives the tenant reasonable time for terminating the tenancy and vacating the premises.

96 Business Tenancies: Terms of the New Tenancy

The terms of the new tenancy may be agreed between the landlord and tenant and in default of agreement are determined by the Court. Thus the Court determines, for example, the duration of the new tenancy and the rent to be paid.

If the Court grants the new tenancy for a term of years certain, the tenancy must not exceed 14 years.

The rent, if determined by the Court, must be such as would reasonably be expected from the letting of the premises in the open market by a willing lessor, but the following considerations should be disregarded:

(a) the fact of occupation by the tenant or his predecessor in title; (the tenant in possession may be prepared to pay an unduly high rent to avoid disturbance of his trade);

(b) any goodwill attached to the holding by reason of the carrying on thereon of the business by the tenant or his predecessor in business;

(c) the value of any improvements carried out by the tenant or his predecessor in title.

The following two conditions must be satisfied for the improvement in (c) not to be taken into account (ie to increase the rent):

(i) the improvement must not have been carried out in pursuance of an obligation to the landlord; and

(ii) that they were completed not more than 21 years before the application for the new tenancy was made.

Before the Law of Property Act 1969 amended Section 34 of the Act, the improvements were disregarded only if they had been carried out during the current tenancy. It often involved injustice to the tenant. If the new tenancy were granted for a short period (as it often was), say for three years, any improvements made by the tenant did not pay for themselves within so short a period. Thus there was a reluctance on the part of the tenant to make improvements, resulting in detriment to himself, the landlord, the business and, in effect, to the community at large. For this reason Section 34 was amended and now the tenant is more prepared to carry out improvements if he knows that (provided the tenancy is extended) he will not face an increased rent for the next 21 years.

There was a proviso under the 1954 Act that the old rent should be paid until the new rent was agreed between the parties or determined by the Court. Inevitably the proviso was an inducement to a tenant facing a considerably higher rent in future to protract the procedure for granting the new tenancy. To make this stratagem futile the Law of Property Act 1969 inserted a new Section 24A into the 1954 Act, in which it is stated that the Court may order the payment of an interim rent, determined by the Court from the date

127

on which proceedings are commenced until the new tenancy is granted and the new rent assessed.

Under the 1954 Act the new rent should have been determined for the whole period of the new tenancy and for this reason the Court was often reluctant to grant a new tenancy for the whole permitted period of 14 years as, due to inflation, this might be inequitable for the landlord. In one case (concerning 88, High Road Kilburn (1959)) the Court granted a new tenancy for 14 years with a proviso that on the landlord's request, the rent might be revised by an arbitrator. This proviso was agreed between the parties and, therefore, not contested, but it is doubtful whether the Court, under the wording of the 1954 Act, would be allowed to make such a determination. The Law Commission recommended allowing the determination of a variable rent and this has been effected in the new Subsection (3) of Section 34 of the Act (amendment made by Section 2 of the Law of Property Act 1969): 'where the rent is determined by the Court, the Court may, if it thinks fit, further determine that the terms of the tenancy shall include such provision for varying the rent, as may be specified in the determination'. The Court may decide that the rent should be increased at stated intervals by a given amount, or provide that the rent should be subject to reference to an arbitrator or Court. Thus it appears that the Court has a very wide discretion, and perhaps now it will be more prepared to grant longer tenancies. This is, of course, in the interest of business and the community.

97 Business Tenancies: Compensation in Lieu of New Tenancy

If the new tenancy is refused on the last three grounds mentioned in § 95, it is obvious that the tenancy comes to the end without any fault of the tenant but with a benefit for the landlord. For this reason in these three eventualities the tenant is entitled to compensation. The compensation amounts to the rateable value of the holding, but if the tenant (including his predecessor in title) has been in occupation for a period exceeding 14 years, the compensation amounts to double the rateable value. Under Section 37 of the 1954 Act compensation was payable only when the Court decided that no Order for a new tenancy should be made. This meant that an application to Court for a new tenancy had to be made, even in hopeless cases, to ensure the right to compensation. The 1969 Law of Property Act gives the tenant a right to compensation in appropriate cases without the necessity of futilely applying to Court for a new tenancy. Thus now the tenant is able to elect to take compensation and quit the holding at the proper time without the need to apply for a new tenancy.

98 Business Tenancies. Contracting out. Jurisdiction
Section 38 deals with the possibility of contracting out of the provisions of the Act.
Two types of exclusions are dealt with:
(a) contracting out of the compensation for disturbance (see § 97);
(b) contracting out of the right to apply for a new tenancy (see § 95).

Contracting out of compensation for disturbance is allowed in cases where the business occupation has been for a period of less than five years by the date on which the tenant quits the holding. There is no objection to an agreement as to the amount of compensation made after the right to compensation has accrued. These provisions, enacted by the 1954 Act, have not been amended.

Contracting out of the right to apply for a new tenancy was absolutely forbidden by the 1954 Act. This was the reason why many stratagems were used to evade the cumbersome provisions of the Act and the amendments enacted by the 1969 Law of Property Act plugged the loopholes in the 1954 version. There may be cases, however, where the landlord does not require the premises for, say, five years but that afterwards he will need them. If there is a tenant who requires the premises for only five years and is prepared to contract out, it is reasonable that such an agreement should be allowed. Therefore a new Subsection (4) was added by the 1969 Act to Section 38 allowing limited contracting out. On the joint application of the future tenant and landlord before the contract has been concluded, or on the joint application during the tenancy, the Court may authorise an agreement for the surrender of the tenancy on such a date or in such circumstances as may be specified in the agreement.

The County Court has jurisdiction over problems pertaining to business tenancies if the rateable value of the premises does not exceed £2000. Otherwise it is the High Court which has jurisdiction (Section 63 of the 1954 Act). Any case may, by agreement in writing between the parties, be transferred from the County Court to the High Court or from the High Court to the County Court specified in the agreement.

Chapter 23

AGRICULTURAL TENANCIES

99 Introduction

This branch of landlord and tenant law contains so many technical provisions comprehensible only to persons possessing considerable knowledge of agriculture that only a short summary of this law, with a stress on procedural aspects is here attempted.

The general law of landlord and tenant also applies to agricultural tenancies, but there are a few rules of Common Law exclusively pertaining to these tenancies. These may be summarised as follows:

(a) there is no implied warranty on the side of the landlord as to the fitness of the land for cultivation. Tenants of agricultural tenancies are supposed to be professional farmers and it is up to them to inspect the condition of the farm (Erskin v Adeane 1873);

(b) the tenant has an obligation to manage and cultivate the land in a good and husbandry-like manner according to the custom of the country. The 'custom of the country' does not imply a universal and immemorial usage (as legal customs do) but only prevalent usage which has subsisted for a reasonable length of time in the neighbourhood. It is usually sufficient to prove such 'custom' by showing that it is so well known and acquiesced to, as to be reasonably presumed to have been tacitly imported into the contract between parties.

This obligation, however, has become much less important in recent times, as there are now many various methods of cultivation recognised as proper ones. This has been acknowledged by the Agricultural Holdings Act 1906 which gave the tenant the right to farm how he pleased, notwithstanding any agreement or custom to the contrary, provided the holding does not deteriorate under his cultivation of it.

(c) The tenant had no right to remove any fixtures at the end of his tenancy. The only exception at Common Law was the right to

131

emblements whereby if the tenancy determined unexpectedly between seed time and harvest through no fault of the tenant, he was entitled to collect the crop he had sown. A general right to remove fixtures under some circumstances was given to the tenant for the first time by the Landlord and Tenant Act 1851. (See § 42).

100 Statutory Provisions

There are a number of Acts dealing with agricultural tenancies, starting with the Landlord and Tenant Act 1851 which was the first Act to deal exclusively with this type of tenancy. This Act gave the tenant the right to remove fixtures if the landlord did not exercise his statutory option of buying them.

The Agricultural Holdings Act 1875 gave the tenant, for the first time, a statutory right of claiming compensation for improvements. Subsequent Acts dealing with these tenancies gave more and more rights to the tenants.

At present, the basic Act dealing with agricultural holdings is the Agricultural Holdings Act 1948 which consolidates previous provisions. This Act, as amended by the Agricultural (Miscellaneous Provisions) Acts 1954, 1963 and 1968, and the Agricultural Acts 1958 and 1970 will be explained in outline.

Before the Second World War the legislature's intention was primarily motivated by the need to protect tenants against exploitation by landlords. In the 1940s, however, the legislature's main concern was to promote and secure as efficient an agriculture industry as possible.

It will be seen that the tenant is well protected against exploitation by demand of an unduly high rent, against losing any investment put into holding and against unnecessary disturbance or termination of the tenancy against his will, but only on condition that he performs his duties conscientiously and cultivates the land in a proper manner.

As the question of the proper cultivation of land and of assessing a 'fair rent' to be paid by the tenant depends on technical and local knowledge of the holding, these questions are better decided by laymen, having extensive knowledge of agriculture and local conditions, than by the Courts. For this reason, as it will be seen, arbitration, or the Agricultural Land Tribunal and not the courts deal, in the first instance, with all disputes arising in this sphere of law.

101 Creation of Tenancies. Limitation of Rent

The Agricultural Holdings Act 1948 defines agriculture very widely, as including horticulture, fruit growing, seed growing, dairy farming and livestock breeding, and the use of land as grazing land, meadow land, osier land, market gardens and nursery grounds and the use of land for woodlands where that use is ancillary to the farming of the land (Section 84(1)).

There is no statutory requirement that all agreements for agricultural tenancies must be in writing, but the 1948 Act provides that if there is no agreement on specified matters (see below) either party may request the other to enter into a written agreement containing all 'specified matters' and if he fails to do so, may refer the terms of the tenancy to arbitration (Section 5 and Schedule 1).

The more important 'specified matters' are:

(a) the names of the parties;

(b) sufficient particulars of the holding;

(c) the period or periods of the tenancy;

(d) the rent reserved and the dates on which it is payable;

(e) liability for land taxes (if any) and rates;

(f) maintenance and repair of fixed equipment;

(g) question of insurance of buildings against fire (usually landlord's obligation);

(h) fertilizing the soil with the full manurial value of harvested crops;

(i) proviso of re-entry on breach of covenants by the tenant.

With reference to (d) if rent is not determined by the agreement between the parties, it is determined by arbitration. Moreover, if the rent had been determined by agreement or arbitration more than three years ago, the tenant (or landlord) may again refer the question to abritration for the determination of the new rent. The new rent, as assessed by arbitration, replaces the existing one from the day on which the tenancy could have been terminated by notice to quit given at the date of reference. Both landlord and tenant may give a notice to quit of not less than one year, but not more than two years before the date fixed for the expiration of the tenancy (Section 3 of the 1948 Act). Thus, practically speaking, the rent of agricultural holdings is subject to review at three-yearly intervals on

133

the initiative of either party.

102 Statutory Provisions Granting Security of Tenure

A letting of an agricultural holding for less than a year (with some minor exceptions) takes effect as a tenancy from year to year. Tenancies from year to year are protected by the Act. Moreover a tenancy for a term of two years or more does not expire at the end of the term but is extended automatically until the statutory notice is given.

The combined result of these provisions is that all tenancies of agricultural holdings are protected with the single exception of tenancies of a fixed length between a year and two years. There would seem to be no policy justification for this and the lack of protection for such tenancies suggests a loophole in the Act. In Gladstone v Bower (1960) the Court accepted that the tenancy for a term of 18 months does not enjoy the protection of the Act (. . . 'If the gap in protection given by the Act is accidental . . . it is for Parliament to remedy the matter').

As was mentioned in § 101, a notice to quit must be given at least 12 months before the date on which the year of the tenancy ends (Section 23 of the 1948 Act), but in the case of the bankruptcy of the tenant the tenancy may be ended immediately.

If a notice to quit is given by the landlord the tenant may, within a month, serve a counter-notice, in which case the notice to quit shall not have effect unless the Agricultural Land Tribunal consents to the operation of the notice (Section 24(1) of the 1948 Act as amended by the 1958 Act Section 8(1) and Schedule 1 Paragraph 8).

In some cases, however, the Agricultural Land Tribunal's consent is not necessary. There are seven such circumstances, the most important being:

(a) if the Agricultural Land Tribunal has consented to the operation of the notice to quit before the notice has been given (the tenant, of course, has an opportunity to appear before the Tribunal by which consent is given in order to put his case);

(b) if the land is required for development approved by the planning authority;

(c) if the Agricultural Land Tribunal certified, not earlier than 6 months before the notice, that the tenant was not fulfilling his responsibilities to farm in accordance with the rules of good husbandry;

(d) if, in spite of a request, the tenant remains in arrears of rent for more than two months after a request has been served, or failed to remedy a breach of another covenant after being given notice of the breach.

(e) if the tenant becomes bankrupt or dies.

The Agricultural Land Tribunal, before granting the consent must be satisfied on a number of points given in Section 25 of the 1948 Act; the most important points are:

(a) that it is in the interest of good husbandry;

(b) that it is in the interest of sound management that the holding should be amalgamated with the estate of which it is a part;

(c) that the greater hardship would be caused by withholding than by giving consent to the operation of the notice.

Thus security of tenure depends on the Agricultural Land Tribunal's views as to the standard of farming of the tenant and hardship caused to either party as a result of their interests being in conflict.

103 Rights and Duties of the Parties on Determination of the Tenancies

The landlord has the following rights on determination of the tenancy

(a) the right to possession of the holding; this right is common to all types of tenancy and does not require commenting upon;

(b) the right to compensation for deterioration of particular parts of the holding (Section 57 of the Act) or for general deterioration of the holding (Section 58).

The claim under Section 57 refers to compensation for dilapidation of, deterioration of or damage to any part of the holding caused by the non-fulfilment by the tenant of his responsibility to farm in accordance with the rules of good husbandry, eg the wrong removal of dung, neglecting repair of buildings, fences and gates, removing landlord's fixtures, etc.

Under Section 58 — general deterioration of the holding — the landlord has to give a notice to the tenant at least one month before the end of the tenancy; here the tenant is responsible for the depreciation in the value of the holding due to deterioration during the tenancy by the failure of the tenant to cultivate the land according to the rules of good husbandry or the terms of his contract. In this case it is not necessary to point out exactly what wrongs have been committed; it is sufficient if the arbitrator finds that the value of the holding has been depreciated due to poor farming, which may evade specification.

The tenant has the following rights on the termination of the tenancy:

(a) the right to remove his fixtures

The right of removal of fixtures is now governed by Section 13 of the 1948 Act. The tenant may remove any engine, machinery, fencing, building of other fixture provided that it can be done without damaging the reversion or provided that any damage may be made good. The tenant, however, has to give a notice to the landlord one month before the termination of the tenancy and the landlord is entitled to purchase the fixtures paying the price agreed between the parties or assessed by the Agricultural Land Tribunal.

(b) The right to emblements

Emblements are crops which ordinarily repay the labour by which they are produced within the year in which the labour has been bestowed (such crops include grain, hemp, vegetables or hops). The right to emblements has been considerably curtailed by Statute and virtually replaced by the 'tenant's rights', enacted in Part II of the 4 Schedule to the 1948 Act (see below).

(c) The right to compensation for improvements

The tenant is entitled to compensation for improvements, hence the incentive for him to improve the holding is maintained. The general principle for assessing compensation is that the compensation must correspond to a sum fairly representing the value of the improvements to the incoming and not the outgoing tenant.

All improvements for which the tenant may claim compensation are fully listed in the 3 and 4 Schedule to the 1948 Act. These improvements are divided into three categories:

(i) Improvements to which the consent of the landlord is required (Part I of the 3 Schedule). These improvements are of a rather permanent nature which change the character of the holding.

There are seven of them, the most important being the planting of hops, orchard or fruit bushes; also works of irrigation.

(ii) Improvements to which the consent of the landlord or the approval of the Agricultural Land Tribunal is required. There are 17 such improvements, which are mostly of a semi-permanent nature, and which may, or may not, be really useful to the holding. Examples of these improvements are: construction of silos, making of improvement of roads and bridges, land drainage, provision of means for sewage disposal, etc.

(iii) Improvements in respect of which no consent is required. These are improvements which should be done in the course of day-to-day cultivation and which do not affect the character of the holding. These include the chalking of land, application of purchased manure (including artificial fertilizers), protection of fruit trees against animals, etc.

(d) The tenant's rights

Part II of the 4 Schedule provides for other matters in respect of which compensation is payable; these matters, however, are not 'improvements' but old 'emblements' (now called 'tenants's rights') established not by custom, but by Statute. Thus the tenant has a right to claim compensation for growing crops, seeds sown and cultivations, pasture laid down by the tenant, etc.

(e) Compensation for increased value of the holding. (Section 56 of the Act)

When the tenant of an agricultural holding shows that by the continuous adoption of a system of farming, the value of the holding has been increased, he is entitled to compensation amounting to the increase in value. This Section, being of residual character, is little used, as it is difficult to prove that the system used by the tenant has really increased the value of the holding.

104 Compensation for Disturbance

Where a tenancy of an agricultural holding terminates by reason of a notice served by the landlord (otherwise than owing to the tenant's death, bankruptcy or default) and the tenant vacates the holding, he is entitled to compensation for disturbance. This amounts to a year's rent, but if the tenant notifies the landlord accordingly and proves higher loss, he is entitled to a larger amount up to two years' rent. Compensation for disturbance is due in addition to any compensation for improvements and cannot be contracted out of.

In this case it is the County Court which decides the amount and orders its payment.

The Agricultural (Miscellaneous Provisions) Act 1968 improved considerably the position of the outgoing tenant. Sections 9 *et seq.*

provide that where a landlord has to pay compensation to the tenant under the Agricultural Holdings Act 1948, he is to pay a further sum equal to four times the annual rent of the holding, the purpose being to assist in the organisation of the tenant's affairs. There are, however, exceptions, the more important being where the Agricultural Land Tribunal consents to the notice to quit by reason of the tenant's default, or where owing to the 'greater hardship' rule the Agricultural Land Tribunal decides the case in favour of the landlord. Under Section 12 of the 1968 Act in cases of compulsory purchase, the acquiring authority has the same duty as if it were the landlord.

Section 12 has no application if the tenant (having two years or more of the tenancy to run) is entitled to full compensation under the Land Compensation Act 1961.

As an alternative to a Section 12 payment, the Land Compensation Act 1973 (Section 35) provides a 'Farm Loss Payment' to tenants of leases granted or extended for a term of years certain of which not less than three years remain unexpired. Freeholders are also entitled to it. As the majority of agricultural tenancies are from year to year it is not often that this payment would be due to tenants. It amounts to one year's profit computed by reference to the profits of the last three years of the tenancy.

105 Jurisdiction

Many disputes arising between the landlord and tenant regarding agricultural tenancies are referred to arbitration by the Acts. The rules covering this are contained in Schedule 6 to the 1948 Act, the 1963 Act and the Agriculture (Miscellaneous Provisions) Act 1972. The arbitrator is a person appointed by agreement between the parties or, in default of agreement, by the Minister from among the members of the panel constituted for this purpose. Neither party has powers to revoke the appointment of the arbitrator without the consent of the other party. The 6 Schedule to the 1948 Act deals with some points of procedure, otherwise the Arbitration Act 1950 applies to the arbitration under the Act 1948 as amended.

A number of matters is referred to the Agricultural Land Tribunal, the most important being: consent to operation of notices to quit, certificates of bad husbandry, approval of long-term improvements, etc. The Agricultural Land Tribunals have been established by the Agriculture Act 1947, extensively amended by the 1958 Act (Section 8 and 1 Schedule). There are eight Tribunals in England and Wales; the chairmen have a legal qualification and two other members are appointed, representing the interests of the owners and tenants of agricultural holdings respectively.

PART III

Short Note on Leases under French and German Law

Chapter 24

FRENCH AND GERMAN LEASES

106 General

The concept that land belongs to the Crown and that other persons may only own interests in the land is unique to the Common Law and unknown in other systems. In Continental systems the land itself may be owned by anybody.

A further basic difference is that under the Common Law tenants have a 'real' right to the land, a right effective against the whole world, whilst on the Continent tenants only have 'personal' rights against their landlords arising from the contract between them. However this idea that tenants have no 'real' rights in the land let to them has been modified by legislature, as will be explained.

Although in the German and French systems land and chattels may be subject to ownership in a similar way, there are, however, some distinctions between movable and immovable things (this division roughly corresponds to the Common Law distinction between personal and real property). The most important distinctions are:

(a) some real rights over somebody else's things are possible only in respect of immovables (eg servitudes and hypothecs); hypothecs are to a large extent equivalents to our mortgages, or, strictly speaking, to our 'charges of land by way of legal mortgage'. Hypothecs may also be created over ships which, in this respect, are treated as immovables;

(b) prescription is governed by different rules; a longer period is required if immovable things are concerned;

(c) 'possessory action', a speedy process for regaining lost possession (an action adopted from Roman Law) is possible only for regaining possession of immovables and not movables;

(d) in the case of immovables the efficacy of conveyance (as regards third parties) depends upon registration of title; in the case of movables it depends upon the transfer of possession;

143

(e) execution in respect of debts if directed towards immovables is much more elaborate and time consuming.

107 Leases and the Protection of Tenants in French Law

As has been mentioned, leases in French Law are regarded as contracts only creating personal and not real rights. As the tenant only has a personal right he cannot acquire the property in land by prescription. Also a possessory action cannot be brought by him (he should notify the landlord if he is disturbed in his possession and ask the landlord to proceed). Exceptionally, if he has been violently dispossessed (such possession is called *reintegrande*), he can bring action himself.

There are, however, some rules which to some extent assimilate the tenant's rights in to 'real' ones. Thus Section 1743 of the *Code Civile* secures the tenant whose lease has been created for a fixed term against expulsion by the landlord's successors in title even if succession was effected for value and the successor acquired the property in good faith. The tenant in this situation is also protected against the landlord's creditors. Since 1955 leases for periods longer than 12 years have to be registered in the register of deeds. Although under the *Code Civil* the landlord may terminate a lease either on the expiration of the term fixed, or by notice, the legislature intervened and granted considerable protection to three types of tenancies (types corresponding closely to those protected by English Law):

(a) business premises;
(b) dwellings and professional premises;
(c) agricultural holdings.

(a) Business Premises

Only leases entered initially for a period over nine years are protected. Protection is very similar to that afforded in England. The tenant has the right to ask for a renewal of his lease, and the landlord may object on certain grounds such as the unsatisfactory conduct of the tenant, etc. The conditions of the extended lease if not agreed between the parties are determined by the Court. The landlord may refuse to renew the lease even if the tenant's conduct is irreproachable, but in this case the landlord has to pay the tenant compensation assessed by the Court.

The above provisions (initially made in 1926, almost simultaneously with the English Landlord and Tenant Act 1927) alter the status of the landlord to that of an investor and, in spite of the theory that there is only a contractual *nexus* between the parties, the provisions give the tenant rights almost equivalent to 'real' rights.

(b) Dwellings and professional premises

Professional premises (ie premises occupied by doctors, dentists, etc, but not industrial or commercial) are treated in a similar way to dwellings.

Legislation, dating from 1918, gives tenants security of tenure and limits the rent in a similar way to that in England. There are the following likenesses: there is a protection of successors if they are members of the deceased tenant's family; the protection does not cover service flats; and protection is denied to tenants who have been offered alternative accommodation.

On the other hand there are differences, the most important being: licencees (ie occupiers) are protected even if they are not proper tenants; there is no distinction between furnished and unfurnished tenancies; the protection applies only to selected towns which are suffering from a shortage of accommodation. The rent is fixed differently than in England, as it is not a standard rent, referred to the rateable value (such a concept does not exist in France), nor is it a 'fair rent' determined by somebody. The basis of determination is the area of the dwelling, but the price is modified by taking into account locality, amenities of the dwelling and financial circumstances of the tenant.

(c) Agricultural holdings

Until the Second World War there was no legislation protecting tenants of agricultural holdings. Before that time a tenant had a rather subordinate position as the landlord could refuse to extend the lease and had a decisive voice in directing the way in which the land should be cultivated.

Now the terms of the initial lease are left to the parties, but in the absence of express agreement standard terms come into operation. Disputes are referred to some kind of arbitration, the 'tribunal' consisting of a professional judge and two representatives, one of tenants and one of landlords. The tenancy, as a general rule, is automatically extended for a period of nine years and the landlord may terminate the lease only in specified circumstances, eg if he wants to cultivate the land himself. If the landlord sells the land, the tenant has a statutory option of pre-emption. There are also provisions covering the problem of compensation for improvements.

108 Leases and Protection of Tenants in German Law

In German Law tenancies of movables and immovables are treated by one Section of the code – *Burgerliches Gesetzbuch*– usually called BGB. In this aspect the BGB follows the principles of Roman Law. A tenancy is a purely contractual relation between the landlord and the tenant. However, in contrast to the position in France, the tenant is the possessor of the property let and as such may defend against any interference with possession (even if it is done by the landlord).

There are, however, rules which apply only to tenancies of immovables. Sometimes they extend to allowing the tenant of immovables to become almost the owner of an 'estate' – if such a concept existed in German Law. The landlord by entering a contract of lease agrees to three implied terms: a warranty of title to let, a warranty of fitness of the premises for contractual use and obligation to repair. There is a concept similar to distress, although differently expressed, namely the landlord has a statutory *lien* in respect of any movable property belonging to the tenant and found on the premises. The analogy is pressed further by giving the landlord a right to trace the property of the tenant even if removed by him from the premises let. Although the lease is supposed to be a mere contract, the tenant maintains his position *vis-à-vis* the purchaser of the property, who is presumed to have stepped into the contractual shoes of the vendor.

After the First World War (again we see here an analogy to the English law) the extreme housing shortage caused the Government to issue special legislation protecting tenants of dwelling houses. The difference here between the English and German system is that German Law comprises three types of legislation:

    (a) control of housing;
    (b) determination of rent;
    (c) security of tenure.

(a) Control of housing

This legislation – going far towards socialization of housing – is

146

unknown to English Law and, therefore, deserves some attention. 'Accommodation Offices' run by the local authorities were created. They registered both persons seeking accommodation and also vacant premises for letting. The latter were registered when vacant even without the consent of the owner. The Offices had the right to allocate tenants to future landlords; usually it was done by submitting several candidates to the owner, who could select his tenant. If he did not do so, the Accommodation Office had the authority to determine the terms of the agreement and allocate a tenant to the landlord. This legislation tried to strike a balance between the conflicting interests of both parties and made hoarding of vacant possession impossible. It served its purpose in the lean years of the German economy between the wars and for some time after the Second World War.

(b) Restriction of rent
This was effected by referring the rent to be charged to the rent paid on 1 July 1914 (the so called pre-war rent of *'Friedensmiete'*, which means 'peace-time rent'). This limitation applied only to old houses and to those erected after the Second World War if built with the help of subsidies from public funds. It did not apply, however, to houses constructed by proprietors themselves from their own funds. There are comparatively few such houses, as, after the war, financial help from public funds was generously afforded for building purposes. In effect some 8 million dwellings were erected in West Germany in the 24 years between 1945 and 1968 (On average 333,000 dwellings per annum).

(c) Protection against eviction
Protection against eviction was given on roughly similar lines as in Britain.

The emergency legislation outlined above was abolished in West Germany in 1968 and in West Berlin in 1970.

Immediately after the war there was also an Act – 'Business Rooms Tenancies Act' *(Geschäftsraummietengesetz)* – of 1952 (which replaced previous, more extensive legislation) which, however, was repealed in respect of West Germany at the end of 1967, in respect of West Berlin at the end of 1968. At present business premises are not protected in any way.

Now in West Germany there is legislation in respect of dwelling

147

houses which reflects the Social-Democratic trends prevailing in West Germany. These may be summarised under the three headings:

(a) rent aid system;
(b) protection against termination of tenancies;
(c) protection against an unreasonably high rent.

(a) Rent aid system

The aim of this system is to help needy tenants in meeting their rent. A certain proportion of the family income is allocated to the payment of rent and, if it is insufficient, the tenant has a right to ask for a rent subsidy. The tenant may be deprived of this subsidy if he is voluntarily unemployed, loses his employment by committing a criminal offence, or if his financial difficulties are a result of excessive spending or drunkenness. These subsidies are more generous than those in this country.

(b) Protection against termination of tenancies

By applying the rule of undue hardship, the Court can order the continuance of the tenancy, taking into account both the circumstances of the tenant and the landlord.

(c) Protection against an unreasonably high rent

On the application of the tenant, if the Court comes to the conclusion that the rent is excessive, it has power to reduce the rent to a reasonable amount, without affecting the other terms of the tenancy.

The *Amtsgerichte,* the lowest Court — equivalent to our County Court — has exclusive jurisdiction over these cases notwithstanding the amount of money involved in the dispute.

BIBLIOGRAPHY

Cohn E. J., Zdzieblo W. *Manual of German Law* 1968 British Institute of International and Comparative Law.

Dobry G. & Barnes M. *Hill and Redman's the Law of Landlord and Tenant* 1970 Butterworth

Fox-Andrews J. *Business Tenancies* 1970 Estates Gazette Ltd.

Lawson F. H., Anton A. R., Neville Brown L. *Amos and Walton's Introduction to French Law* 1966 Oxford University Press

Lloyd D., Montgomerie J. *Business Lettings* 1956 Butterworth

Luderssen K. *Planning and the Legal System in Germany* 1971 International and Comparative Law Quarterly 20 Part I.

Macmillan S. K. *Law of Leases* Estates Gazette Ltd.

Megarry R. E. *The Law of Real Property* 1966 Stevens & Sons Ltd.

Morris J. H. C. *Property Statutes* 1972 Sweet & Maxwell.

Neville Brown L. *Comparative Rent Control* 1970 International and Comparative Law Quarterly 19 Part II.

Nevitt B. *Housing in West Germany* 1966 Local Government Chronicle, May 1966.

Walton R., Essayan M. *Adkin's Landlord and Tenant* 1973 Estates Gazette Ltd.

West W. A. *The Concise Law of Housing* 1965 Estates Gazette Ltd.

INDEX

References are to numbers of paragraphs, not pages.

155

Appendix A

RENT ACT 1974

Under the legislation existing prior to the Rent Act 1974, protection in respect of dwelling houses was of two kinds, one for unfurnished tenancies, another for furnished lettings. The line between the two was often very blurred and arbitrary, particularly since unfurnished tenancies became, in 1965, subject to 'fair' rent, whereas furnished lettings were subject to 'reasonable' rent (Sections 46 and 73 of the Rent Act 1974).

The Rent Act 1974 changed the principle distinguishing these two types of protection. Generally speaking, greater protection, (virtually identical to the protection under Part IV of the Rent Act 1968 given to unfurnished regulated tenancies) has been afforded to tenancies, where the tenant lives in 'purposely built blocks of flats', or in flats where the landlord does not reside in the same building, irrespective of whether the tenancy is unfurnished or furnished. Lesser protection (that given under Part VI of the Rent Act 1968 to furnished lettings) has been afforded to tenants living in flats (but not in 'purposely built blocks of flats'), where the landlord resides in the same building, again irrespective of whether the tenancy is furnished or unfurnished. This system applies fully only to tenancies created after 14 August 1974, as unfurnished tenancies created before that date still enjoy full protection (even if the landlord resides in the same building), because otherwise they would be deprived of their vested rights.

Accommodation 'shared' with the landlord remains protected to the limited extent as furnished tenancies.

In carrying out the policy explained above the Rent Act 1974 in Section 1 provides that a dwelling house shall no longer be prevented from being a protected tenancy by reason *only* that the dwelling is bona fide let at a rent which includes payment in respect of use of furniture. Thus furnished tenancies have generally been transferred from the protection of Part VI of the 1968 Act into Part IV, which

161

deals with regulated tenancies. Consequently we now have 'protected furnished tenancies' and 'statutory furnished tenancies', and also 'protected unfurnished tenancies' and 'statutory unfurnished tenancies'. However, only unfurnished tenancies may be controlled; furnished ones may be only regulated and not controlled. (Limited protection, under Part VI of the Rent Act 1968, is exceptionally retained if the tenancy (furnished or unfurnished) is provided together with board or attendance).

Further, three types of furnished tenancies are exempted from protection under Part IV of the 1968 Act and still remain protected as they have always been under Part VI.

Firstly the most important exemption has been introduced by adding a Section 5A to the Rent Act 1968: A tenancy will not be protected if the following three conditions are all satisfied:

(a) the dwelling house forms part only of a building and that building is not a purposely built block of flats; and

(b) the tenancy was granted by a person who, at the time that he granted it, occupied as his residence another dwelling house which also forms part of the building; and

(c) not only at the beginning, but also during the tenancy, the landlord occupied as his residence a part of the building. This condition, however, is mollified in three circumstances:

 – on the sale of the premises, an interval of up to 14 days is disregarded and if the purchaser occupies the premises within 14 days after the vendor vacates, the continuity is not broken;
 – if within the above 14 days the new owner notifies the tenant that he will move into the premises, then the period is extended up to six months;
 – if the owner dies and the premises are vested in the personal representatives, the period is extended to 12 months.

Secondly a tenancy for a holiday period is not protected either under Part IV or Part VI of the 1968 Act (Section 2(1)(bbb) and Section 70(5) of the 1958 Act).

Thirdly tenancies granted to students by a specified educational institution or body are not protected. A statutory instrument 'the Protected Tenancies (Exceptions) Regulations 1974' S.I. 1974/1366 provides that such institutions are universities, polytechnics, colleges of education etc.

There are two rather important provisions, aimed at the prevention of evasion of the Act. A landlord cannot deprive a tenant

162

of protection by moving into residence and then granting a new tenancy. Also, if a tenancy is granted for a fixed term (and is thus not protected), a second tenancy for a fixed term granted by the same landlord to the same tenant would be protected.

Grounds for possession in Schedule 3 have been amended, in particular a case 3A has been added: 'ill-treatment of furniture by the tenant'. A further case 10A introduces the new ground of recovery of possession by owner who acquired premises with a view to occupying them eventually on retirement, if he gives a notice of this intention at the beginning of the tenancy or, in respect of existing tenancies within six months of the coming into operation of the Act. There are also provisions for obtaining possession of premises let for a short-term between holiday period or between school terms.

There are a number of consequential amendments to the Rent Act 1968, but dealing with them in a detailed manner is beyond the scope of this note. The most important points are:

The Rent Tribunal's jurisdiction is retained for:

(a) owner-occupied landlord letting — even unfurnished;
(b) all other matters except those tenancies which have now become furnished protected tenancies;
(c) sharing accommodation;
(d) accommodation with board and attendance.

The Rent Tribunal may now not only decrease, but also increase the rent. Parties may submit their cases to the Rent Tribunal every three years, or even within the three months preceding the expiration of three years period.

The Rent Tribunal's registration of the rent of furnished tenancies (if they have been converted into protected tenancies) now counts as registration by the Rent Officer; consequently the grounds upon which an application for re-registration of rent may be made includes the case of regulated furnished tenancies, where the quantity, quality or condition of the furniture has undergone change. The quality etc of furniture is to be considered in determining a fair rent.

It is within the county court's jurisdiction to decide whether a furnished tenancy is protected or not.

The protection of furnished tenancies is extended to those whose rateable value either was before 1 April 1973 £400 in London or £200 elsewhere, or has been since 1 April 1973 £1500 in London or £750 elsewhere.